Old Man On His Back

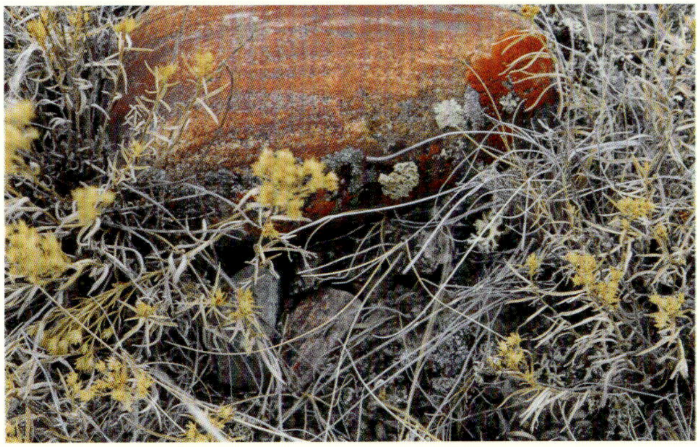

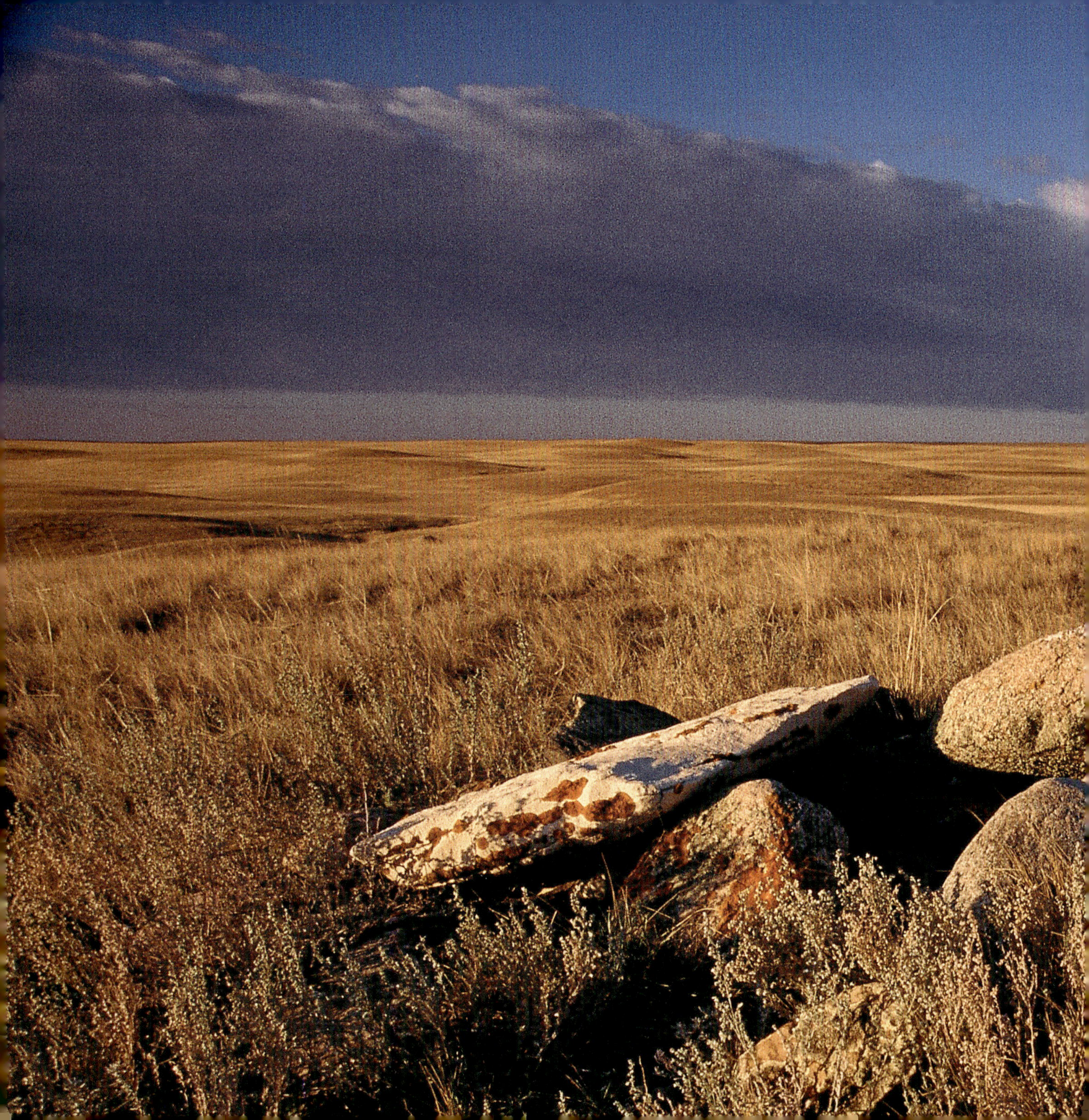

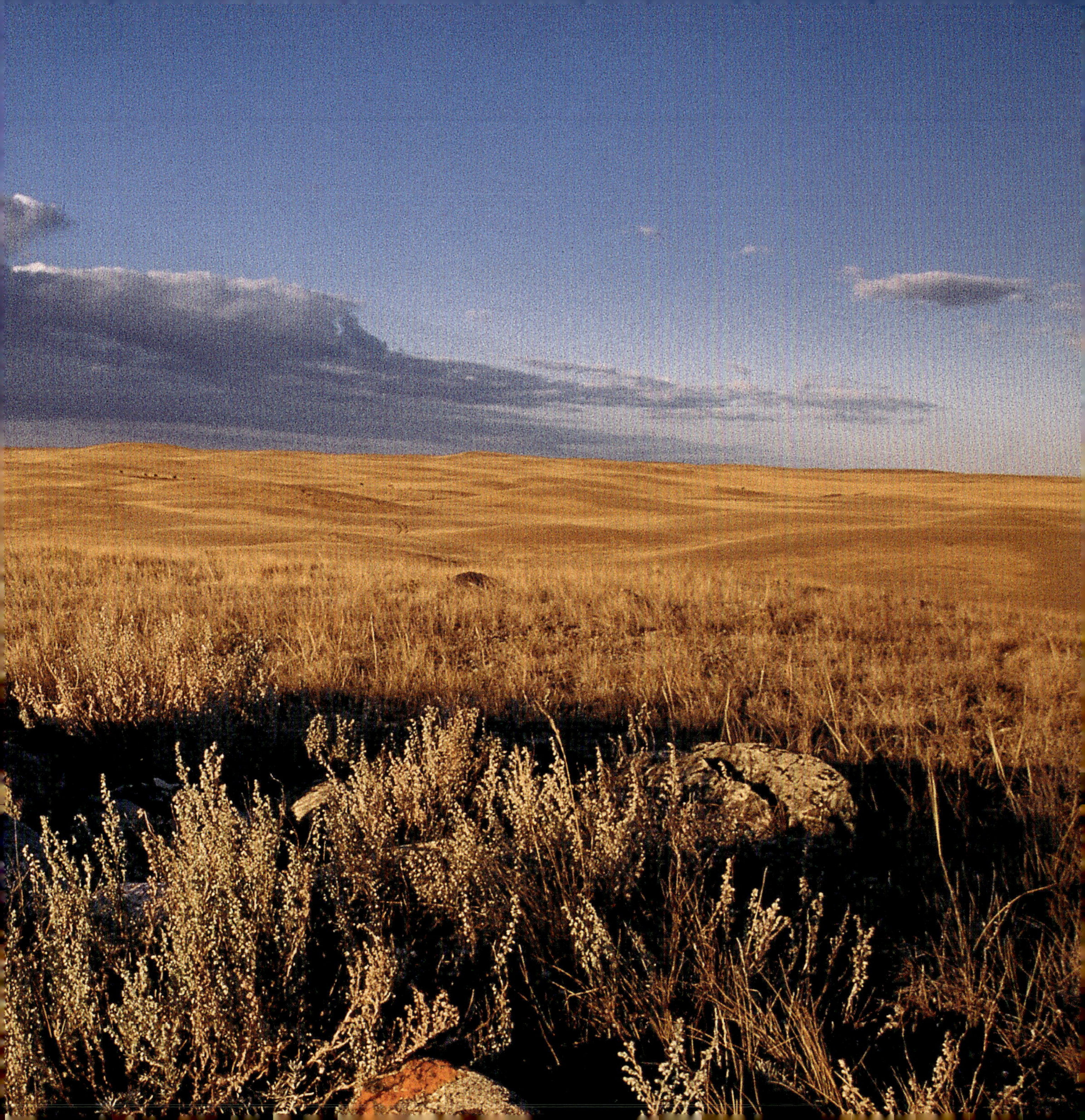

TEXT BY
SHARON BUTALA

PHOTOGRAPHY BY
COURTNEY MILNE

OLD MAN ON HIS BACK

PORTRAIT OF A
PRAIRIE LANDSCAPE

HarperCollinsPublishersLtd
A PHYLLIS BRUCE BOOK

NATURE CONSERVANCY
CANADA

Old Man On His Back: Portrait of a Prairie Landscape

For information address HarperCollins Publishers Ltd, 55 Avenue Road, Suite 2900, Toronto, Ontario, Canada M5R 3L2

www.harpercanada.com

HarperCollins books may be purchased for educational, business, or sales promotional use. For information please write:
Special Markets Department, HarperCollins Canada, 55 Avenue Road, Suite 2900, Toronto, Ontario, Canada M5R 3L2

First edition

Canadian Cataloguing in Publication Data

Butala, Sharon, 1940–
Old Man on His Back : portrait of a prairie landscape

Co-published by the Nature Conservancy of Canada.
"A Phyllis Bruce book".
ISBN 0-00-200085-7

1. Old Man on His Back Prairie and Heritage Conservation Area (Sask.) – Description and travel.
2. Old Man on His Back Prairie and Heritage Conservation Area (Sask.) – Pictorial works.
I. Milne, Courtney, 1943–
II. Nature Conservancy of Canada.
III. Title.

QH77.C3B88 2002 917.124'3 C2002-900558-2

DWF 6 5 4 3 2 1

Printed and bound in Canada
Set in Monotype Garamond

p. i: *Lichen, clubmoss, dried broomweed and short curly grass are characteristic of the OMB prairie.*

pp. ii and iii: *On some of the highest hills, Aboriginal stone cairns remind passers-by of the area's human history.*

pp. iv and v: *The very vastness of the prairie offers a sense of freedom.*

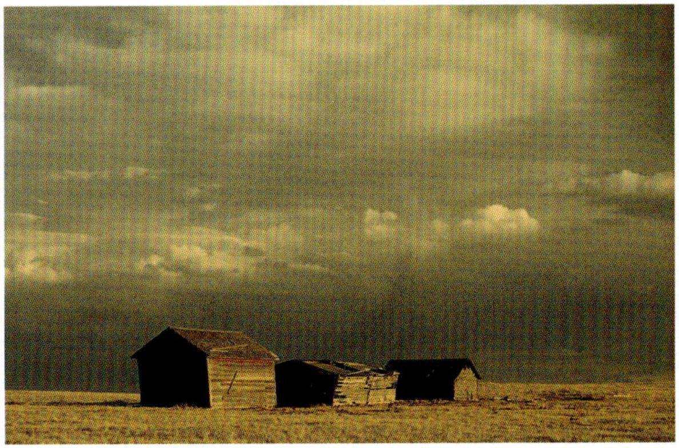

Contents

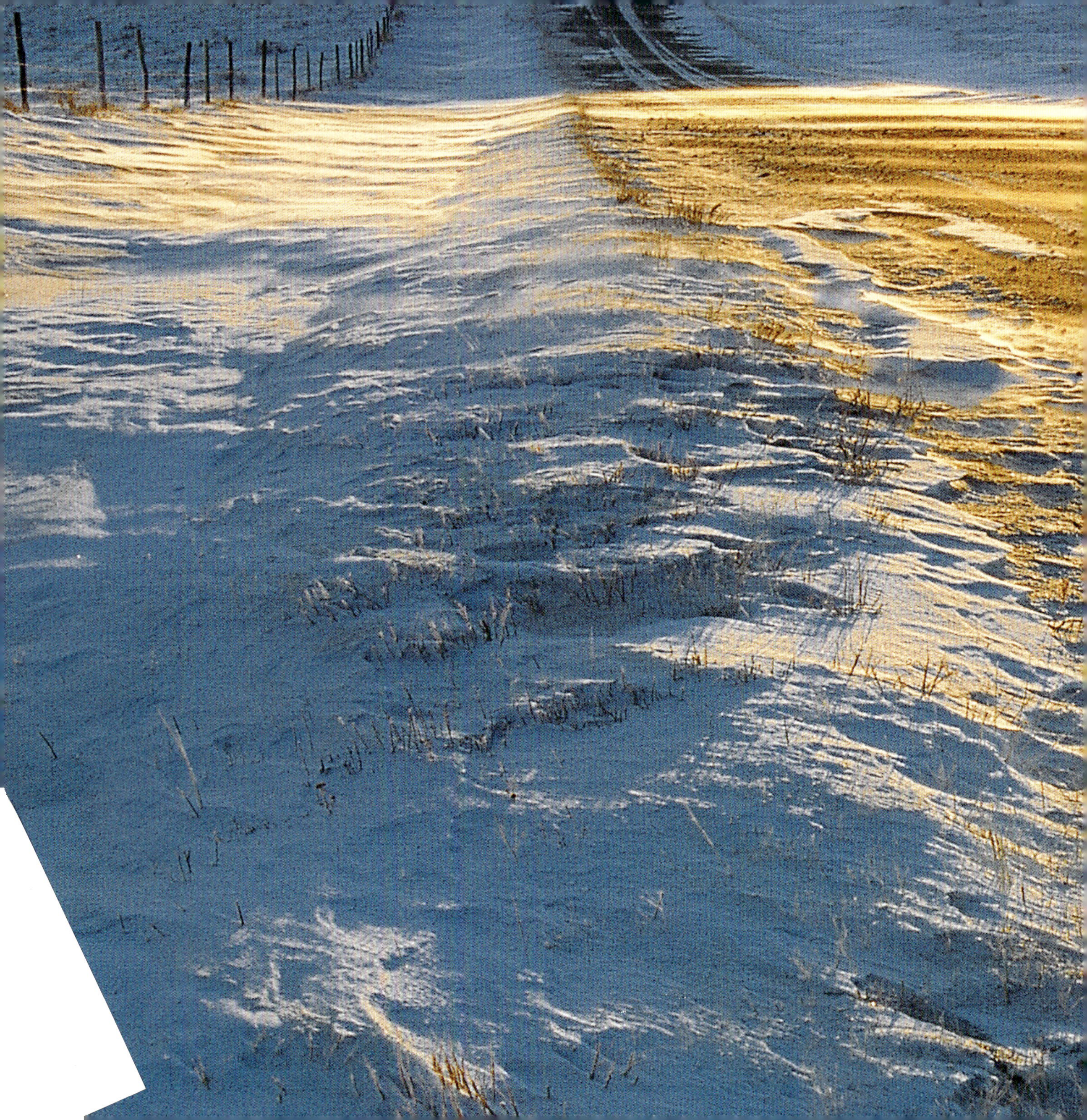

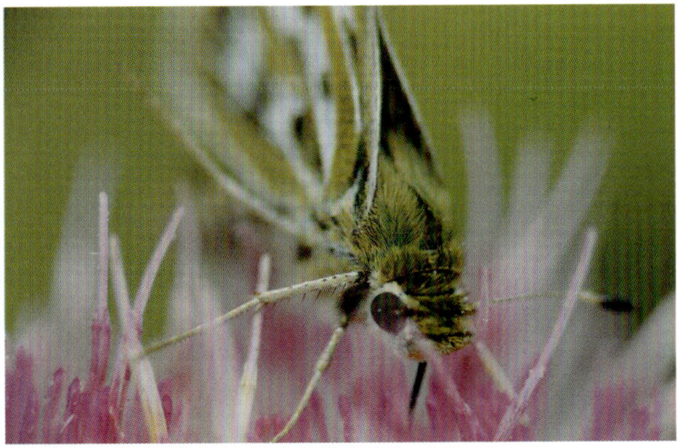

FOREWORD

This book tells an extraordinary story.

It tells the story of a family's commitment to the land, to the careful stewardship of its natural values, and to its ongoing preservation for generations to come.

It also tells the story of a magnificent achievement for Canada. Of 13,000 acres of almost untouched prairie that have been saved forever. Of an expanse of rolling hills and gently shifting grasses that will never see construction of homes, never be ploughed for crops. A wealth of pristine beauty that will be allowed to continue in its natural rhythms, offering shelter and sustenance to the many imperiled plants and animals that call it home.

Left: In a near-desert country, and with the changing climate, snow is rarely abundant.

The showy blooms of the thistle, where most prairie flowers are tiny, provide sustenance to larger insects.

The story of the Old Man On His Back Prairie and Heritage Conservation Area (OMB) is told here by Sharon Butala and Courtney Milne. Their words and pictures work together to create a powerful image of this conservation success story, and to bring into focus the beauty and rarity of this unique piece of Canada.

Located in southwestern Saskatchewan, the OMB is the Nature Conservancy of Canada's flagship grassland project. Situated between two large blocks of intact native grassland primarily owned and managed by the Crown, the 13,000 acre project completes a nearly contiguous block of native prairie more than 200,000 acres in size. With less than 30 per cent of the original mixed-grass prairie remaining in Canada, this is a significant achievement.

The area was secured in 1996, when Peter and Sharon Butala began the process with a donation of 1,000 acres of their own property to the Nature Conservancy of Canada—what was the Butala family ranch. Thanks to their careful stewardship of this property during their ownership, it is one of the best remaining intact expanses of semi-arid mixed-grass prairie.

But making the OMB a reality went far beyond the Butala donation and the grateful acceptance of the Nature Conservancy of Canada. Its securement is the result of an extraordinary collaboration of government, corporations, the local community, and conservation organizations.

The partners who made the purchase of this remarkable preserve possible include Saskatchewan Environment and Resource Management's Fish and Wildlife Development Fund, SaskPower, Environment Canada, the Saskatchewan Wildlife Federation, the Eden Foundation, and many individuals. Saskatchewan Environment and Resource Management, SaskPower, and Environment Canada have also made major commitments to the OMB's ongoing stewardship and care along with the W. Garfield Weston Foundation, Nexen Canada Ltd, Monsanto Canada, IPSCO Inc., Husky Energy Inc. and TD Friends of the Environment Foundation.

For the publication of this book, we owe special thanks to SaskPower for its support. With the long-term viability of the project in mind, SaskPower provided seed money for a stewardship endowment for the OMB, and the start-up funds for this book project, the proceeds from which will go to build that endowment. SaskPower has been a steadfast partner and supporter of the OMB project at every stage and should be commended for its ongoing commitment to the project's success, and to the communication of that success to others across Canada.

The initial work may be behind us, but the OMB project itself is far from

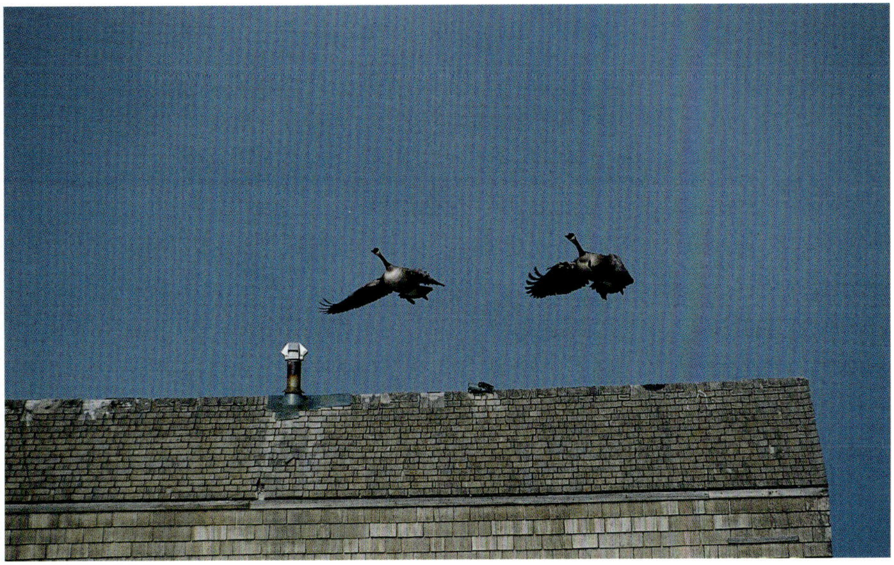

Flocks of Canada geese stop on the OMB during their annual migration.

complete. Designed not as a static conservation project but one that can be used to showcase the positive relationship between agricultural land use and conservation, there are ambitious plans for the OMB. Current plans include: restoring approximately 1,000 acres of previously cultivated land back to native prairie; reintroducing Plains bison as the natural grazer in the area; and preserving the area's cultural value by documenting the archaeological and historic resources, restoring the existing homestead era buildings, and ultimately constructing a visitor centre. All these plans are being put into place in cooperation with the local community and project partners, with the aim of making a contribution to southwestern Saskatchewan's rural economic development. Fundraising to support these initiatives is ongoing.

The OMB is just one example of a conservation success story made possible by the NCC and its partners. There are many equally astonishing stories across Canada. But there are many more places of stunning beauty and biodiversity that still need our protection.

Canadians are often lulled into feeling that the vastness of our nation will protect our natural landscapes from irreparable damage or loss. The reality is, however, that many of Canada's richest and most diverse natural regions are in very real danger of *disappearing forever.*

The prairies—one of Canada's defining natural features—are one of the most severely impacted landscapes in the country, to the point that less than one-half of 1 per cent of the spectacular tall-grass prairie remains. The rich landscapes of Carolinian Canada, which once covered most of southwestern Ontario, are home to one-third of all Canada's rare, threatened, and endangered species, many of them found nowhere else in the country. But Carolinian Canada is on the verge of extinction, with less than 10 per cent of this ecosystem remaining today. Our country is home to 25 per cent of the world's wetlands, one of the most valuable ecosystems we possess in terms of wildlife habitat and value for humans. But in settled parts of Canada, about 90 per cent of all wetlands have been drained.

For anyone with a love for nature and a passion for the Canada of lakes and streams, mountains and plains, the protection of the OMB gives us cause for celebration. At the same time, it must also give us pause for more serious reflection. This is one small success in our efforts to save Canada's natural heritage. Much more remains to be done, and done quickly, if our children and their children are to enjoy a world as rich and beautiful as the one we inhabit today.

As the president of the Nature Conservancy of Canada, I am thrilled that we have been able to bring you the OMB story in this remarkable book. The powerful combination of Courtney Milne's images and Sharon Butala's words will give Canadians a dramatic insight into the beauty and diversity of this prairie landscape, and into the need for its conservation. We hope you will enjoy this visit to Old Man On His Back, that you will share your copy of this book with friends, and that it will inspire you to become part of the effort to save Canada's most precious places.

JOHN LOUNDS
President
The Nature Conservancy of Canada

The Nature Conservancy of Canada

The Nature Conservancy of Canada is a non-profit organization that takes a business-like approach to land conservation and wildlife preservation. Its plan of action is to build partnerships and develop creative conservation solutions with any individual, corporation, community group, conservation group, or government body that shares its passion for habitat protection. Since 1962, NCC and its supporters have protected more than 1.67 million acres across Canada, conserving significant portions of some of Canada's most endangered landscapes, and providing habitat for numerous species at risk.

NCC has eight offices across Canada. For more information, or to become a supporter, call 1 800 465 0029 or visit www.natureconservancy.ca

Our Thanks

The Nature Conservancy of Canada would like to extend its thanks to the numerous donors who have made the ongoing protection of the Old Man On His Back Prairie and Heritage Conservation Area possible. In addition to the following major contributors, many more individuals have donated their funds and time to support this important work.

Peter and Sharon Butala
Eden Foundation
Environment Canada
Husky Energy Inc.
IPSCO Inc.
Monsanto Canada
Nexen Canada Ltd. (Wascana Energy Ltd.)
Saskatchewan Environment and Resource Management, Fish and Wildlife Development Fund
Saskatchewan Wildlife Federation
SaskPower Corporation
TD Friends of the Environment Foundation
The W. Garfield Weston Foundation

Following pages: The gentle slopes of the OMB hills suggest timelessness and peace.

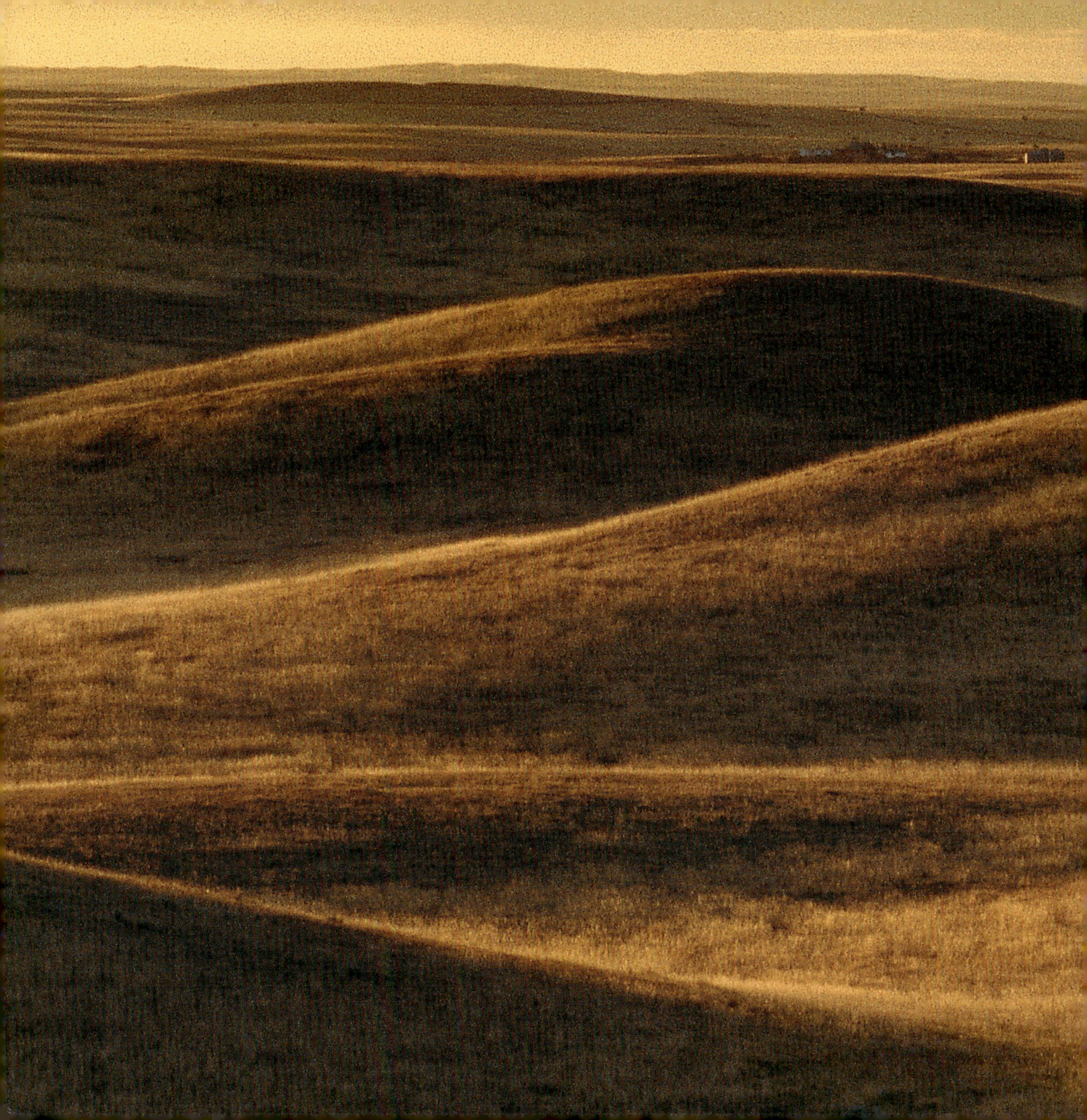

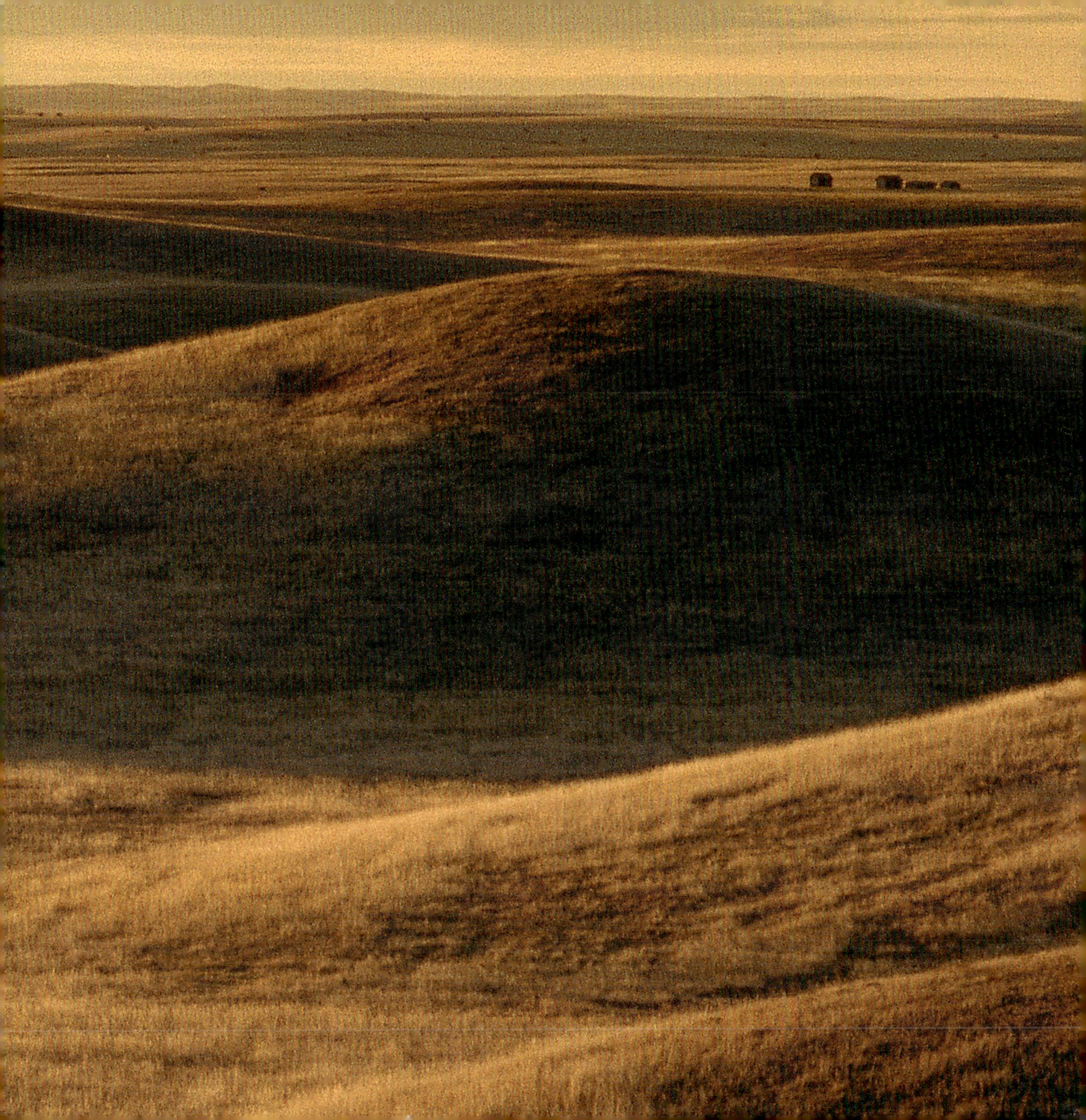

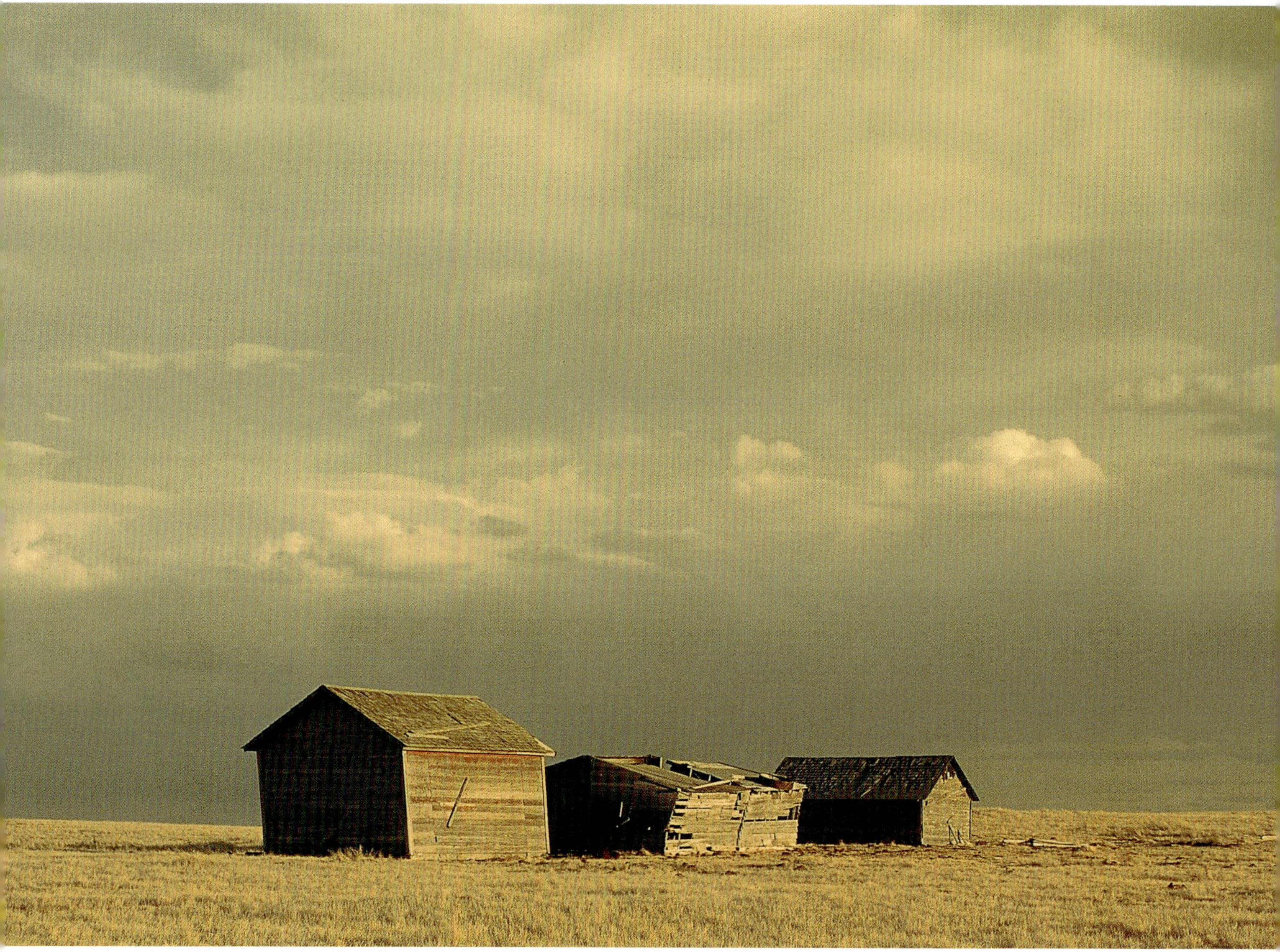

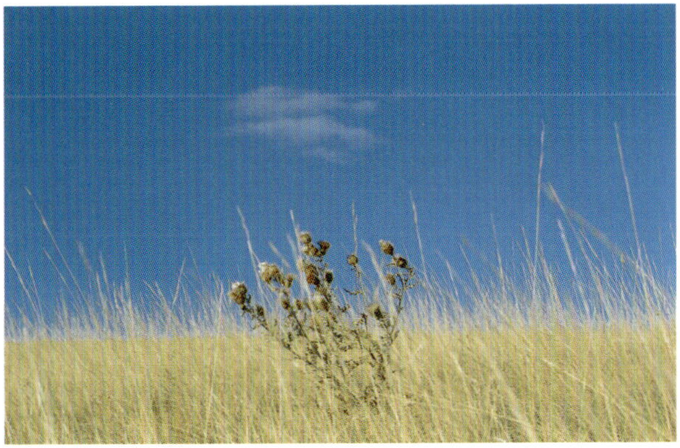

A Place of Peace

To the untutored eye the Old Man On His Back Prairie and Heritage Conservation Area, or OMB—originally the Butala ranch—is a vast area of rolling, grass-covered hills and plains and not much else. A traveller passing through on the dirt road that bisects it from east to west and then turns south to meet Highway 18 perhaps will see a few buff-and-white antelope grazing on a distant hillside, or a coyote trotting past on a meandering path, its nose and tail dropped to the ground. A meadowlark will call, or a few horned larks will rise upward from the grass in short darting flights, like the notes on a bar of music, then drop as quickly to settle again, out of sight. Or maybe an eagle will appear, soaring effortlessly until it's a black dot against the sun, or a hawk will scream, a falling note, and dive, rising moments later with its prey—a mouse, a gopher, a snake—in its claws.

Standing motionless to observe all this, the traveller, the tallest object on the plain, will notice the steady, uneven wind, now a tempest threatening to topple him like the spar of a storm-driven ship, now a gentle breeze that tugs his hair, or like an expert tailor, smooths his clothing delicately against his body. He'll notice the way the whistle or whisper or hollow whoop

Left: The remnants of settlement huddle together bravely in a sea of prairie.

A wavy-leaved thistle, native to the region, rises above the mixed-grass prairie.

changes the sound of other things—now you hear them, now you don't—and, winter or summer, chases the light and shadow across the ice-glazed or sun-parched hills.

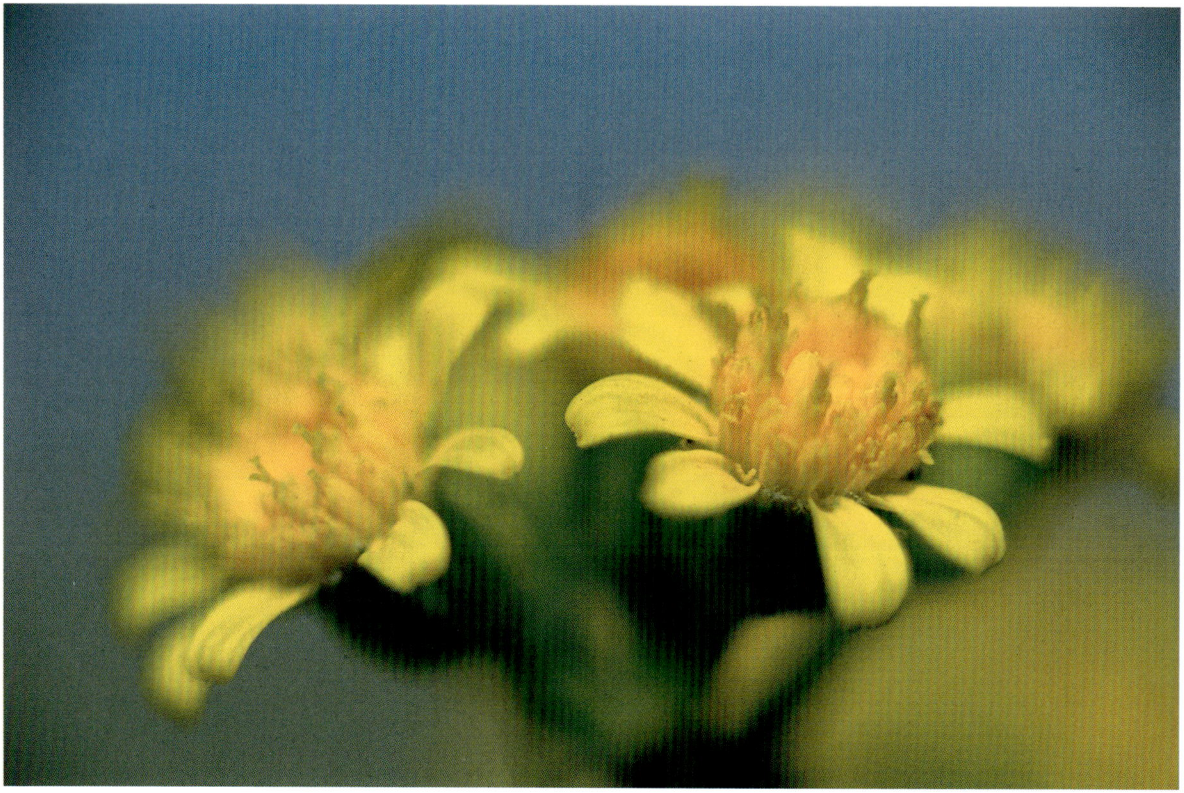

The glowing yellow of the broomweed is characteristic of many of the prairie flowers.

Visitors to the Butala ranch have been overwhelmed not only by the beauty, but by the quality of peace found there that is not necessarily found in other more dramatic landscapes: impenetrable dark forests, wide, rushing rivers, waterfalls, cliffs and sheer rock faces, and soaring, snow-capped peaks. The OMB hills have long, gently curving slopes, which quiet the mind and soothe the heart. For most of the year the hills are a pale gold, varying to tones of buff, cream, beige, and copper, and at sunrise and sunset, tinted shades of rose and gold, or mauve and a luminescent blue. In dull winter light they're coated with silver, and on sunny days they gleam a polished white that, as night descends, turns to indigo and purple. In spring, those same fields and hills are the palest blues and greens, and shimmer gently in the rising heat, the skyline a gently wavering band of blue-green light that invites the traveller to walk to it, and on into some other world of perfect peace and beauty. Such is the OMB: a place where the human soul may find both its roots and renewal.

Mirages, too, are a feature of daily life there in any season, occasionally spectacular and strange—upside-down, or of views of towns thirty miles away—but most merely a vista of plains or hills that without this trick of light can't actually be seen from the viewer's vantage point. They never cease to cause delight, changing the landscape entirely as they do—a delight tinged with wonder that the world could be so amazing and so beautiful.

Imagining a world completely overrun with oil wells, highways, manufacturing plants, potash and coal mines, garbage dumps, and parking lots, we realize that without beauty our souls shrivel, we lose track of who we are as human beings. Even a "brave new world" such as we see in movies or on television where everything—clothing, food, housing, landscapes—is the product of human intervention, human choosing, with all shreds of wilderness safely contained and controlled, all purely natural elements erased, causes us to realize that humans crave a link with nature, with wilderness, with land left as the eons of geological change have created it.

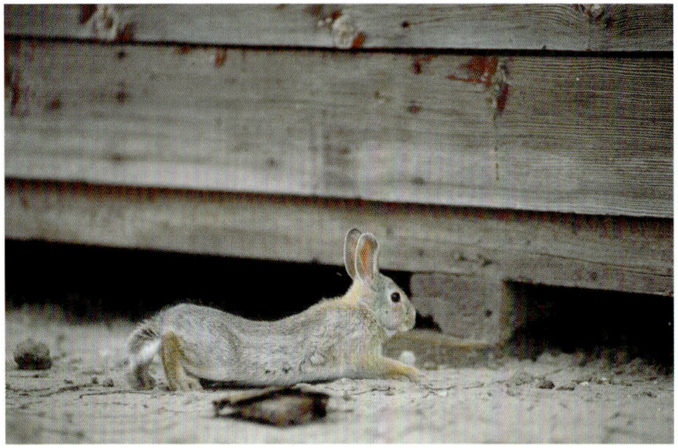

Walking

I came into this place—I like to say that I came into the landscape to live—when I was already in my mid-thirties. I came as a new bride into a world about which I knew virtually nothing, and into a landscape I had not even known existed in Saskatchewan, despite my having lived nearly all my life here. I think now, although I'd never have admitted it then, nor for years afterward, that I married this stunning landscape as much as I married Peter. To live in such beauty seemed to me nothing short of a gift from God.

I hadn't bargained for the difficulties of an urban, single-parent academic marrying into rural agricultural life. I often felt that people were speaking another language—although they all spoke English—and for years I could not even get a grip on how to be a person, a woman, in this strange environment, for all my training had been to live an urban life. I lost my footing then; I fell into confusion; as the years passed I sometimes hovered on the brink of despair.

I had thought that I would live in beauty. I had not conceived of what that beauty consisted beyond endless vistas of grassy hills, a sky so vast that early settlers—women—sometimes went mad and ran from it until their

Bush rabbits (Nuttall's cottontail) nowadays are nearly always found around buildings.

Right: These old cedar fenceposts have withstood nearly a century of bitter prairie winters.

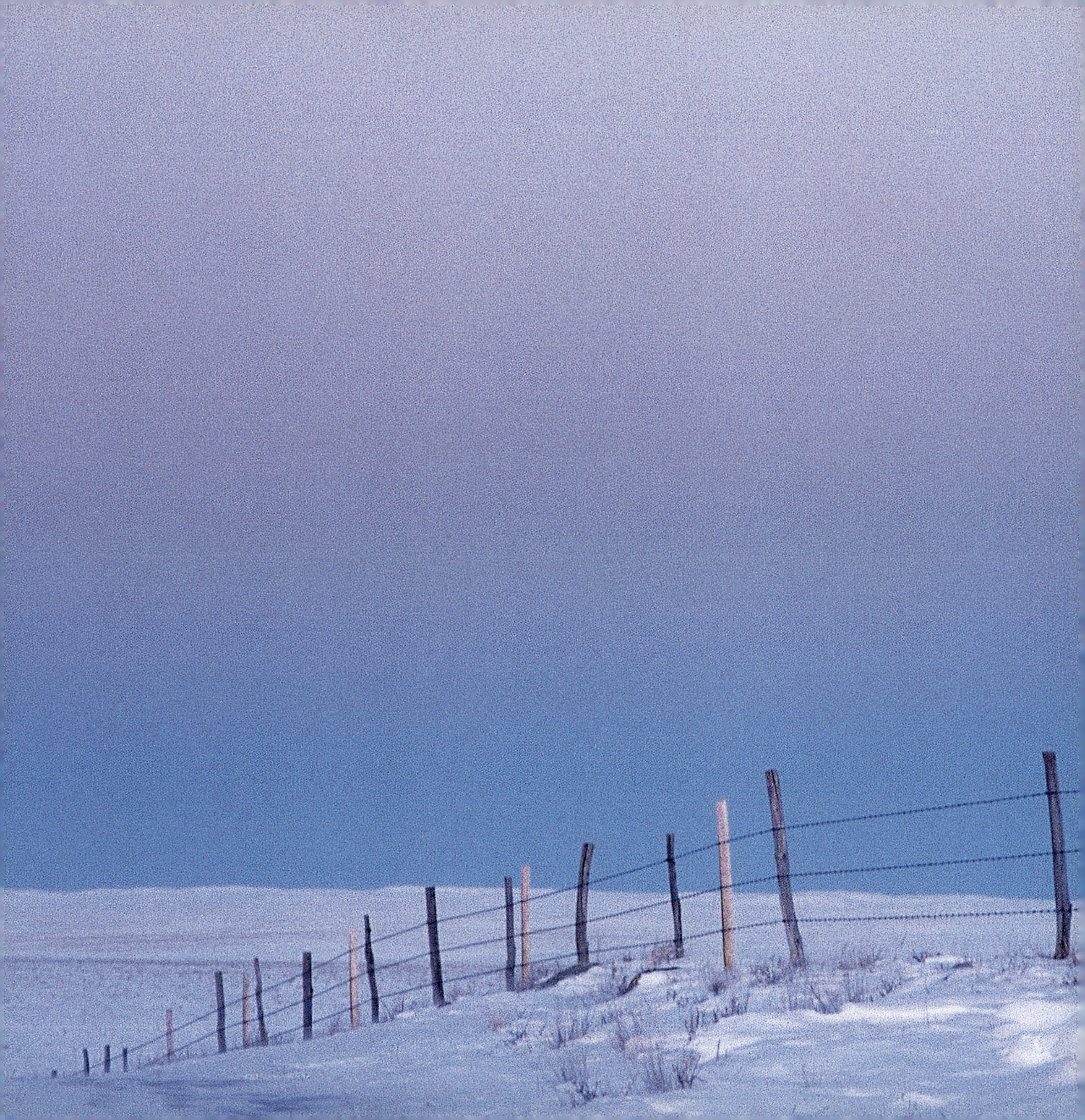

lungs burst and they died, and living life in time with nature's slow rhythms, the arcs of the sun and the moon, the stars wheeling overhead, blazing with light in a silver-haunted, indigo night.

On a ranch occupying an area of about four miles by five miles, as with the settlers, I was the only woman for miles in any direction. In my frequent (and eventually overwhelming) solitude I began to go for walks on the prairie. It was something I could do that didn't require special knowledge, or special equipment, or a companion. I walked because the four walls of our settler's-shack home offered me nothing but a past I hadn't been part of and couldn't understand, and that could not be changed by me to fit an urban standard of home. Time hung heavy on my hands; I walked.

Little clubmoss (prairie selaginella*), magnified here many times, has the vital task of covering the soil to help prevent wind and water erosion.*

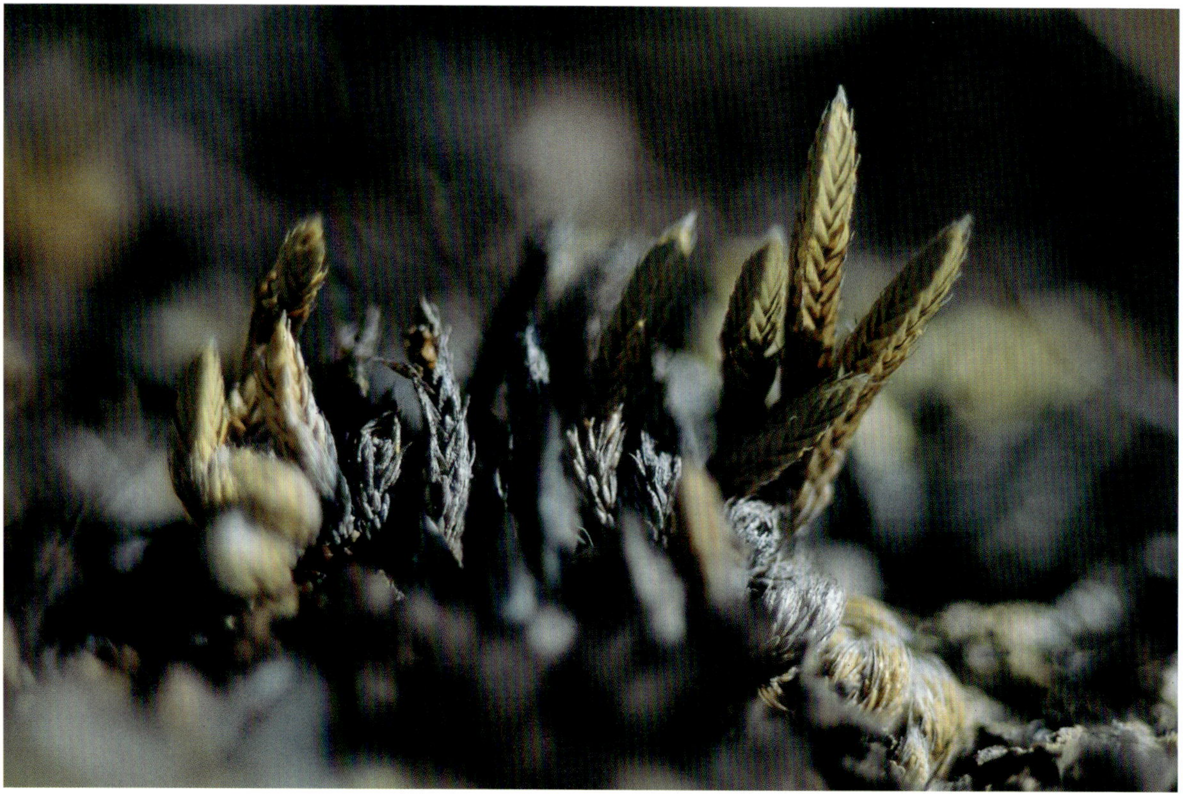

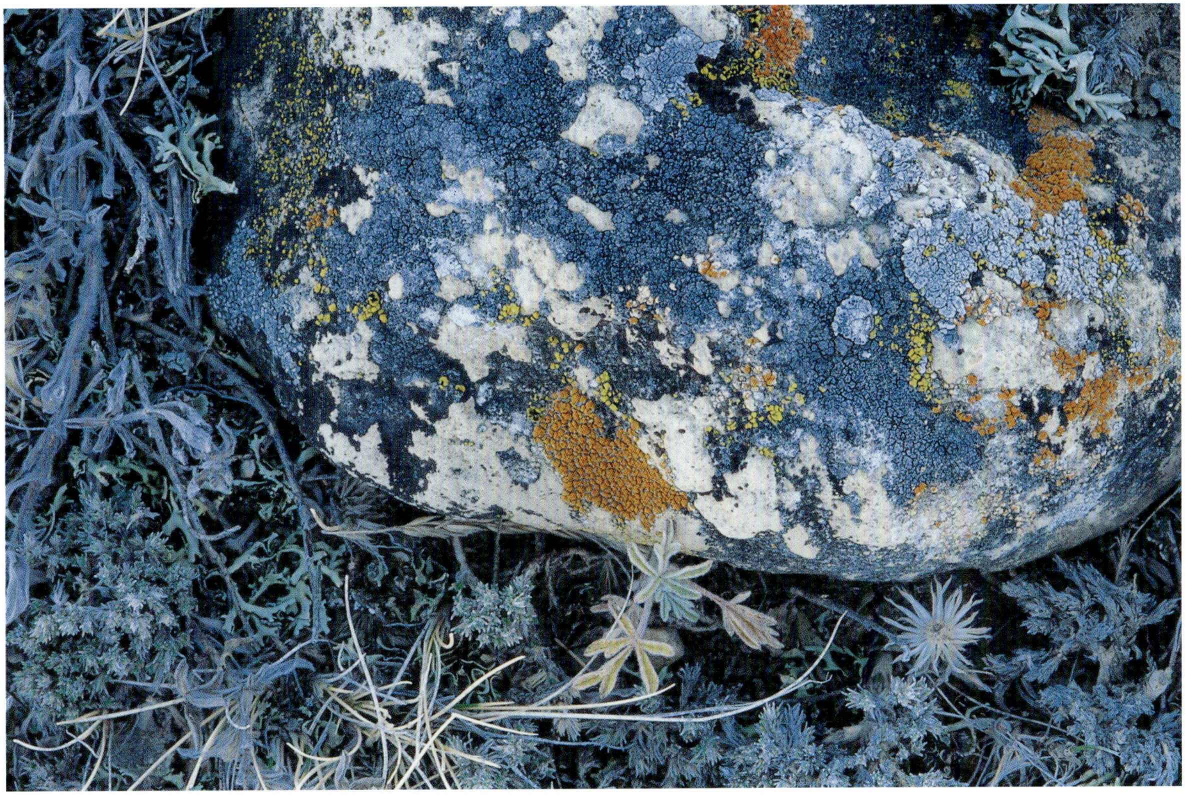

Lichens are both algae and fungi and live on air and rock in a symbiotic relationship.

My mother-in-law, driving out to the ranch one day from the town of Eastend where she'd retired, came upon me as I walked. She said, "It's been a long time since a woman walked this prairie." There was an echo in her voice, of some life I knew nothing about, an emotion that I couldn't find a word for, but couldn't forget, either. I was surrounded by the past, not just the recent homesteading past, her past and her family's past, but farther back, the ranching past, the past of Aboriginal hunter-gatherers, and before that, the past of the glaciers, of the eons of geological time that had brought us all to the moment in which I found myself, a solitary woman, walking the endless prairie.

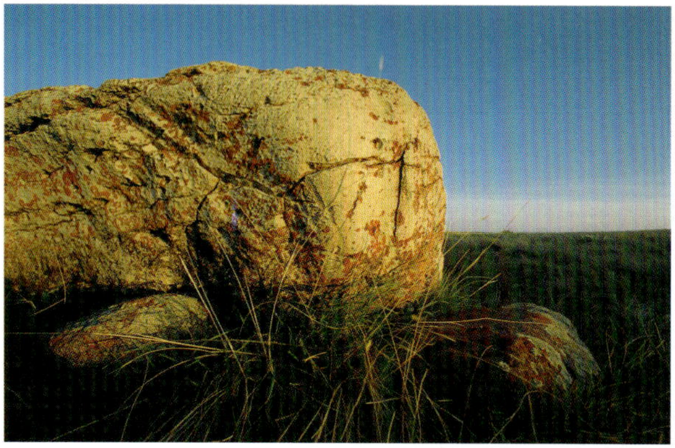

In the Beginning . . .

The Bible tells us that in the beginning there were the waters of chaos moving in darkness; scientists say, just as poetically, that there was rock and collision and a fiery birth from stardust; Aboriginal people say variously that there was a rock, the juices out of which became the world and all that is in it, or that Skywoman fell onto the back of a turtle which was the world, or that Wisahketchahk sent a muskrat down to the bottom of the primal sea to bring up soil from which Wisahketchahk made the earth.

Eons passed, according to the scientists' story, as the stardust consolidated into a misshapen globe. Oceans began to form, and continents to emerge, and what would become Saskatchewan began its northward drift, for a time even lying north of where it is today, until by 1.5 million years ago it had shifted into its present position, with its southern boundary at 49 degrees north latitude and its northern at 60 degrees. Just ten miles north of the 49th parallel a traveller will arrive at the southern boundary of the Old Man On His Back Prairie and Heritage Conservation Area. On clear days, turning to face the south, from the hills of the OMB the traveller will see the low peaks of the Bears Paw Mountains of Montana resting gently on the

This large bison rubbing stone, a soft rock having been stranded on the prairie by glaciers, is called an "erratic."

Right: At moments such as these, the great mystery of the prairie strikes awe in the human heart.

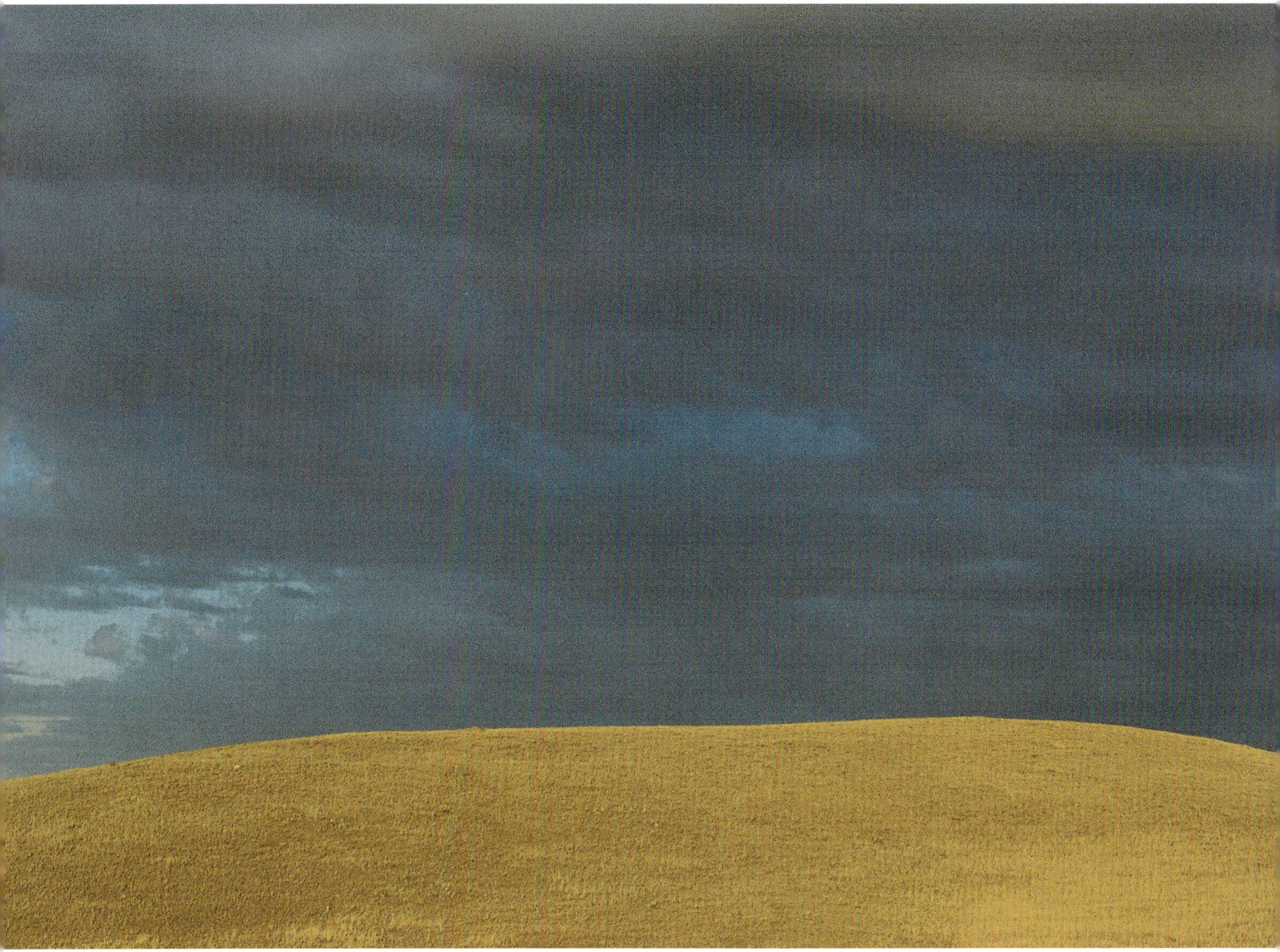

horizon. Or should the traveller come down from the north and turn back to face the way she has come, a dark smudge of resonant blue-purple on the high horizon will remind her that that way lies—for centuries a sanctuary for both humans and animals—the fabled Cypress Hills.

I came to the Butala ranch from the northeast, seeing first the openness of the land, and feeling, at that first sight, all my worries recede beyond my reach in the face of the sheer overwhelming presence of so much nature. I relaxed, I calmed down, I felt a touch of awe always with me at what seemed to me to be the *otherness* of it, mixed with the bewildering knowledge that I had come from it and that it couldn't be other than I was. Nature had returned to me with the full force of her power and, once I got over being constantly stunned by this new sense of what nature is that I couldn't even quite articulate, I puzzled and puzzled over what it actually was besides dirt, grass, stones, sky, moon, sun, and stars. In an agricultural world where grass was to fatten cows, or to be turned upside down in order to grow something else, where land was money and power and prestige, I felt sure there was something else. But what was it? What was land—nature—for? How should I fit with it? How did I fit with it, or in it?

Once I'd come to the ranch to live, I, who couldn't remember dreaming at all, began to have vivid, beautiful dreams. The first of these was probably the greatest, and it isn't an exaggeration to say that it changed my life. In the dream it was night and I was standing at the door of the old ranch house, looking up at the sky where an eagle was soaring. It was so huge that its outspread wings covered the entire ranch yard of about forty acres. The palest beige and cream, with slender, stylized wings and body, it was the most beautiful creature I'd ever seen. But on the cement square in front of me stood an owl that must have been six feet tall. It was a creamy white mingled with grey, and on its breast there were evenly spaced, fan-shaped markings in a deep turquoise and dark grey. The owl was every bit as beautiful as the eagle, and it seemed to want to join me on the porch. Yet, I tried to hold it out while I watched the eagle soaring above.

The far-ranging space of the prairie can deceive the traveller into miscalculating distance.

Although over the years I continue to find new meanings for it, many of which have to do with the eagle and the owl as symbols for the masculine and for the feminine in the world, I believe that the dream was stirred into existence by the new life I was leading in that old ranch house in the midst of miles and miles of prairie in its natural state. The dream happened because every night as I went to the outdoor toilet I walked under a sky brilliant with stars, the very history of the universe riding on my shoulders; it happened because the presence of the moon and her monthly passage had become part of my life; it happened because I began to live each day according to the rising of the sun and its place along its arc through the heavens until it set on the other side of the sky. The lives of birds and animals began to fit in for me with the seasons, and I began to get a sense of the way the chain of life operated. Most miraculously of all, I could understand my womanhood in the light of the rhythms of nature, as part of nature.

Thus, after my busy life in the city and at the university, walking all day on cement, asphalt, and tile, my feet rarely touching the earth, living largely indoors, my entertainment movies, television, house parties, when I returned to nature (having lived in it as a child), its effect was so powerful that it stunned open all my senses and toppled me into a new vision of the world: the mythic world of the human species opened to me. And having been so altered, I opened and became another person, one with much wider boundaries and a far greater sense of my humanity, and yet with a sense of my humanity as merely a tiny part of a whole so great that its extent and boundaries seemed limitless.

I was out of place in my new world, struggling for my footing, my experiences on the prairie and my new dreaming combining to shake me out of any placidity and, yet, mystifying me. I believe now that I thought that if I studied the prairie itself, and learned the social and cultural history of its inhabitants, maybe even learned a tiny bit of science about the landscape in which I now lived, I would get a kind of control over it, as I felt I had been in

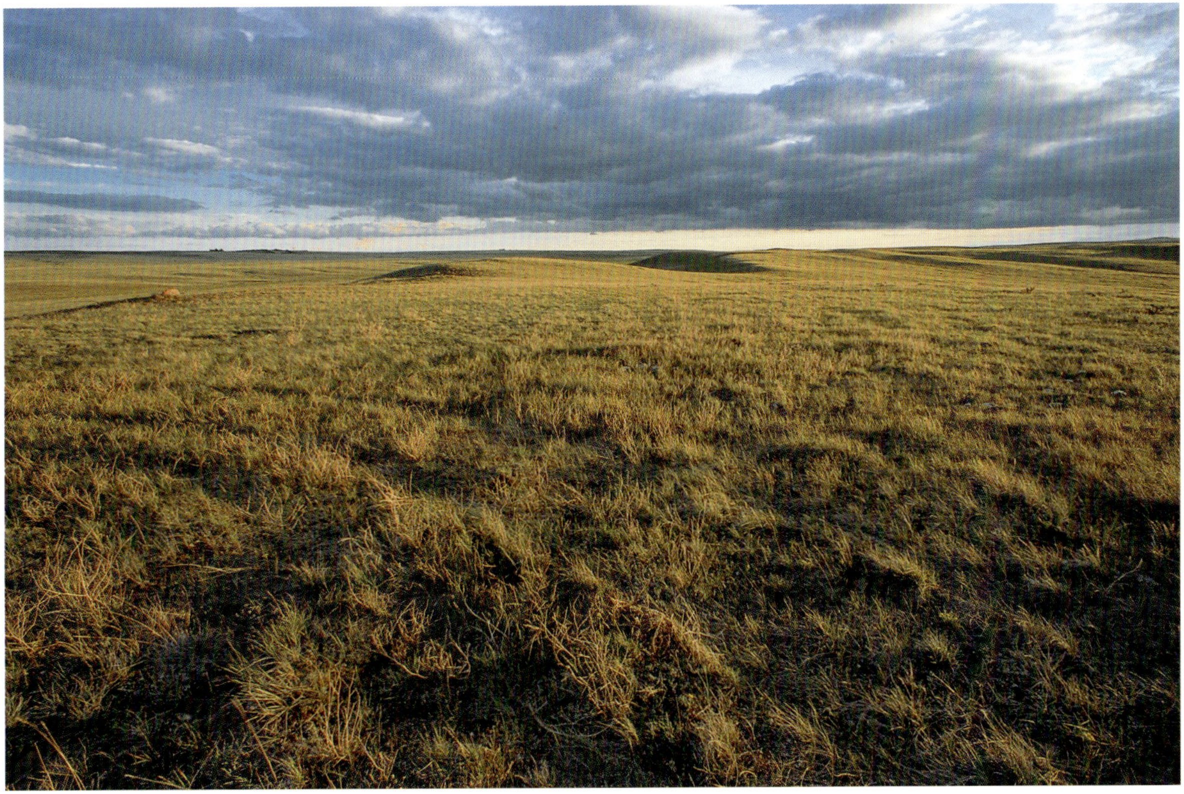

Tracks on the prairie may be as old as a hundred years, revealing the fragility of the grassland.

control of my urban environment. If I understood it in all these ways, surely it would be mine then; I would understand the conversations I overheard, I would understand the people and the land, and I wouldn't be lost any more.

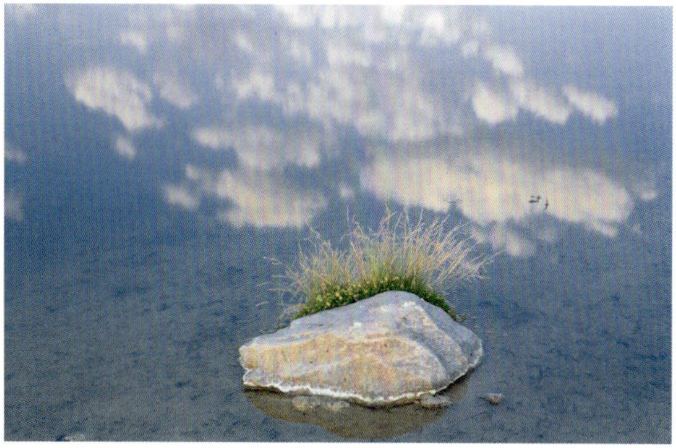

What Is the Meaning of Land?

At the end of the twentieth century and beginning of the twenty-first, I was hardly alone in asking: *What is the meaning of land?* It is turning out to be the central question of the new millennium. As much of the earth becomes increasingly polluted and destroyed or changed—free-flowing water harnessed and diverted for various purposes such as filling swimming pools and watering natural deserts, ancestral forests chopped down, grasslands ploughed—many of us, as we gaze out over our homelands, are quietly, independently of governments, and of universities, and often even of the new environmental agencies, studying this question.

All the years I walked the prairie and puzzled over the nature of nature, I was also reading, searching for the answers in books. First, I wanted to know specific information, but gradually my studies led me from facts about my new landscape into the answers given by various groups in society to this great question. Most interesting to me was the answer of the Aboriginal people of the world still living or remembering their traditional way of life on the land. The answer of those who make their lives in agriculture—farmers and ranchers and all the variations within those two categories, including

Clouds are reflected in spring water.

specialists in range management or crop production or plant genetics—was already fairly clear to me because I was living in their midst. The answer of scientists—botanists, biologists, zoologists, ecologists, and those who specialize in insects or plants or snakes or birds in particular—I found the most baffling because they seemed to be missing entirely what I was coming to see as the most important dimension of nature: the spiritual. The answer of ecologists and other scientist-conservationists, and even of those who call themselves "deep ecologists," seemed closer to an acceptable truth to me, although often I didn't understand them, and more often found them too dogmatic and extreme. The answers of city dwellers—acreage owners, campers, birders, hikers, rock lovers and rock climbers, plant lovers—often

Mists at dawn burn off as the sun rises.

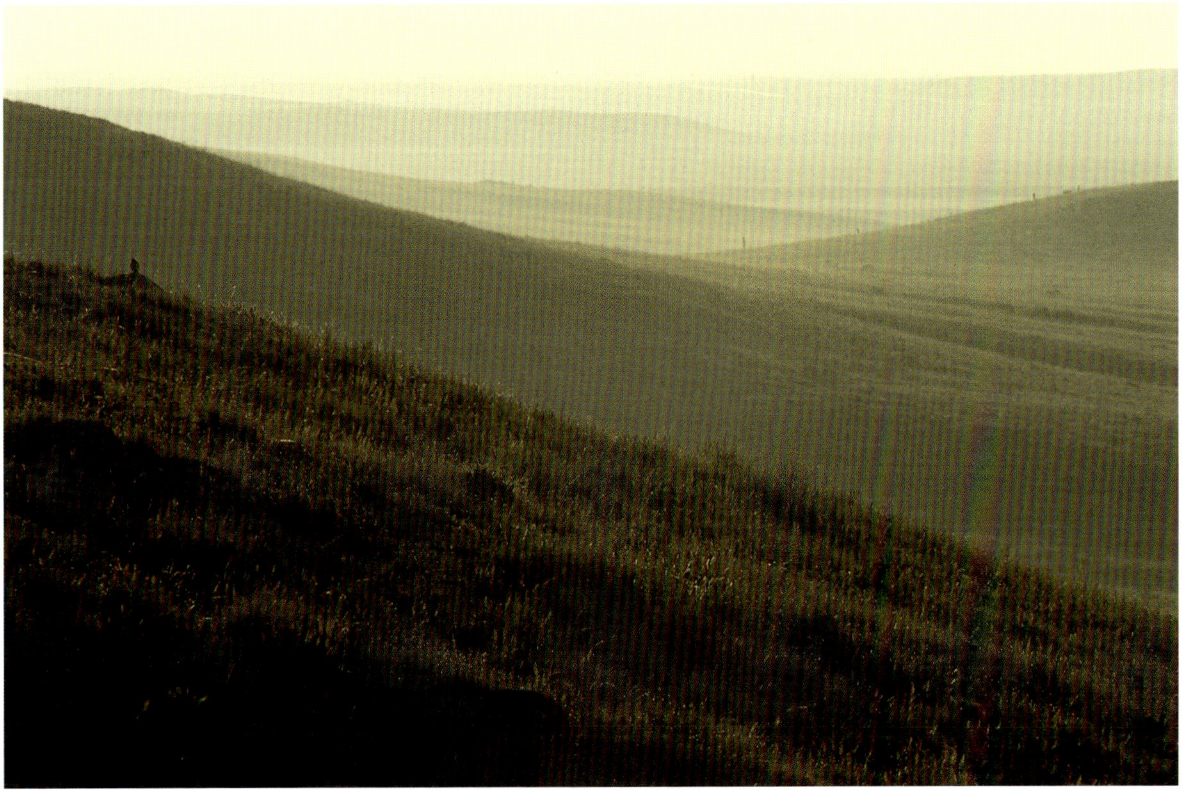

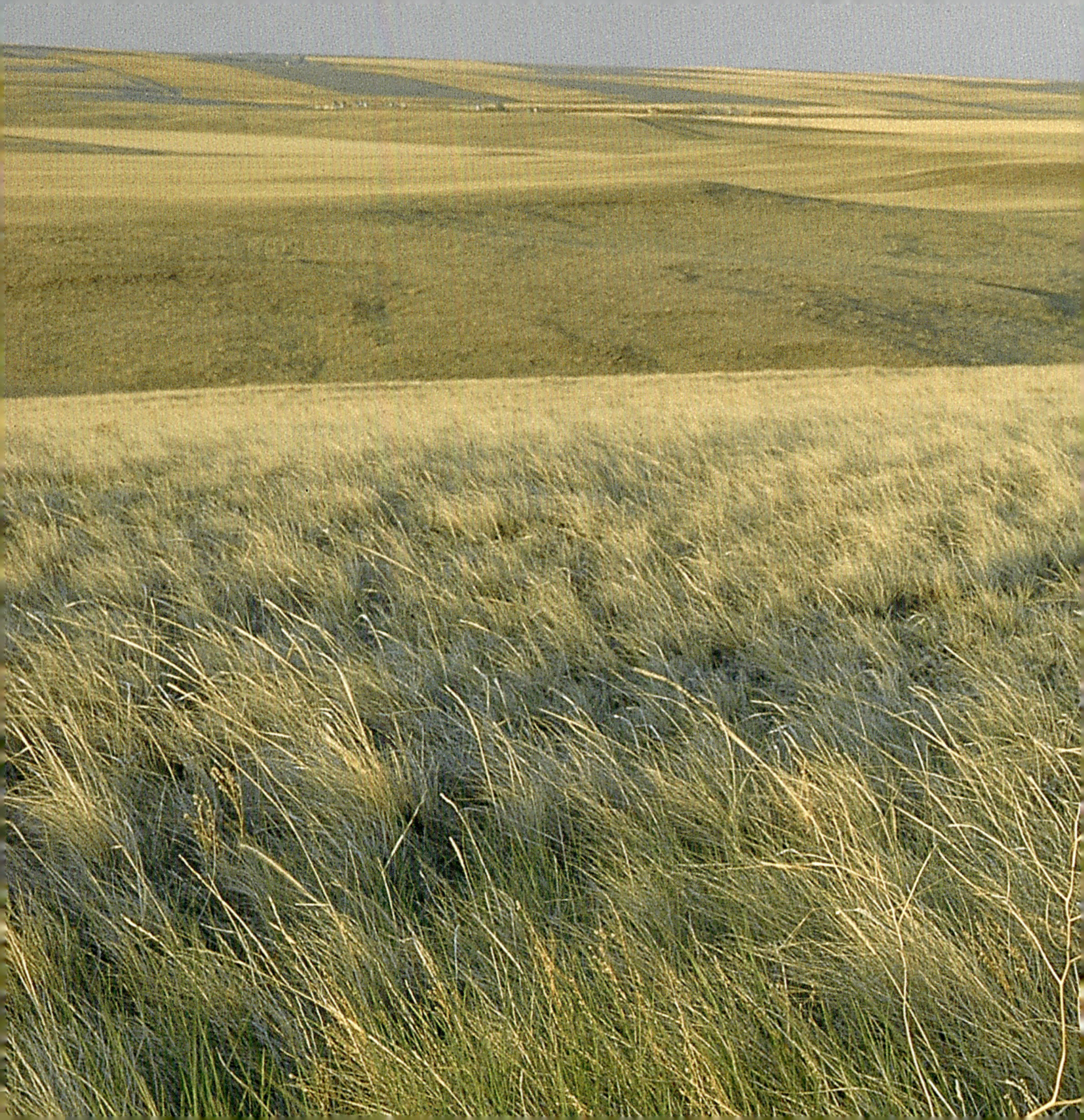

seemed to be focusing too much on the trees and thus missing completely the forest. I was looking for answers, explanations about the experiences I was having in nature, and no one I read or heard had answers that seemed at last to explain everything.

Left: Mixed-grass prairie that hasn't been overgrazed is a welcome and valuable feature of the OMB.

Still a common sight on the OMB, small herds of pronghorn antelope have made their home here for thousands of years.

But I wasn't alone. It is true that with globalization of markets (and even cultures), with extreme degrees of technological application to all sorts of problems, and with a vastly increased population, all of us recognize the need to somehow forge or discover an answer appropriate to this new age, and one on which we can all agree. From all these competing views of land, we have to filter such wisdom that is still viable and necessary to the well-being of all life on the planet.

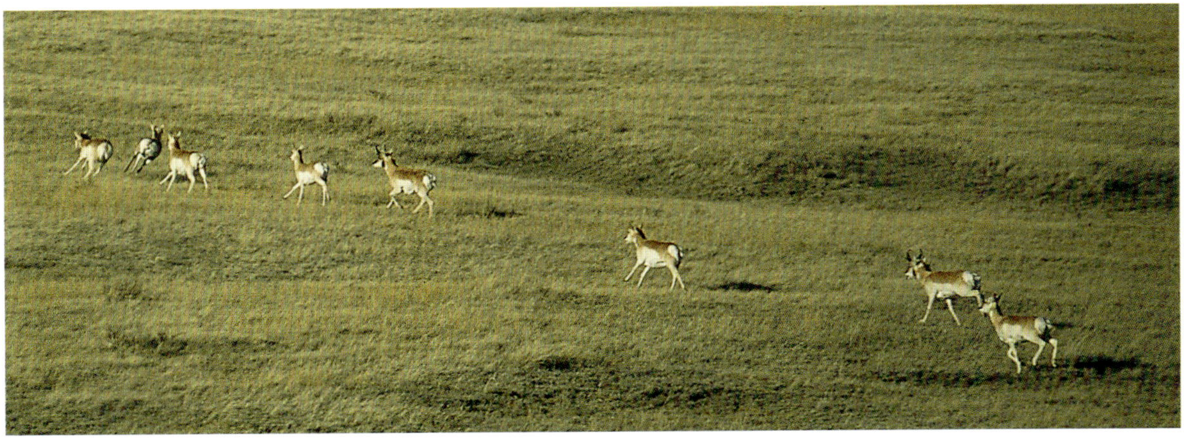

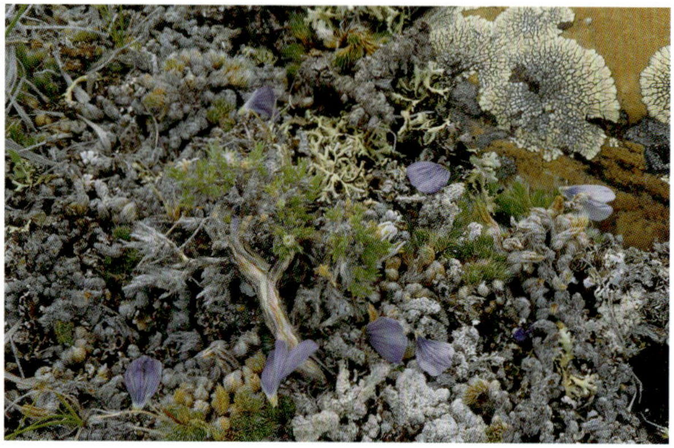

Looking Backward

If I now proceed in an orderly manner to lay out the history of the land that has become the Old Man On His Back Prairie and Heritage Conservation Area, it is not because this is the way I learned it. Not at all. It came to me piecemeal, a little of this mixed in with a little of that, first how to chase a cow, as the cowboys say, and then that jelly can be made from cactus berries, then that Siksika people once hunted here, and then that making a living in farming is a precarious business, and lastly, the first: the geologic processes that formed the grasslands I now called home.

Although the OMB rests on tertiary period bedrock, the topography that I walk across is the result of the glaciations of the last 1.5 million years. During this time, sheets of ice advanced over the area and melted back at least five times, each glaciation more or less erasing the results of the previous one (except for the Cypress Hills, which remained above at least the last sheet of ice), until approximately 14,000 years ago when the last glaciation, the Wisconsin, melted back in the OMB region. The ice left behind a vast plain, the Great Plains of North America, that extends from the Gulf of Mexico into Alberta and Saskatchewan. Here, in southwestern Saskatchewan, on the

The wild blue flax flower sheds its small petals on the rough clubmoss and moss phlox.

Right: A fisheye lens view of "Big Sky Country."

Following pages: The famous prairie light, captured in early morning, creates a new landscape for this mule deer.

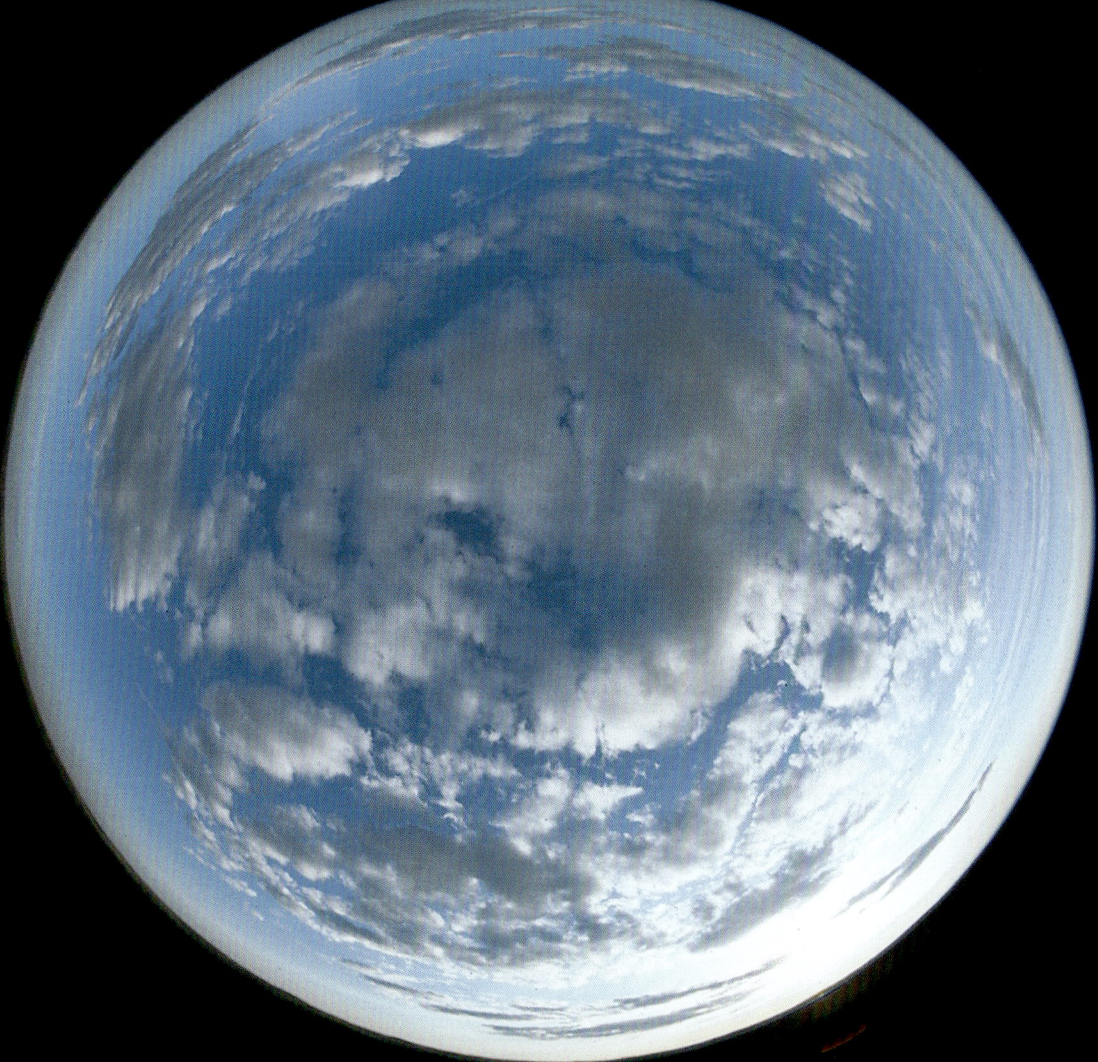

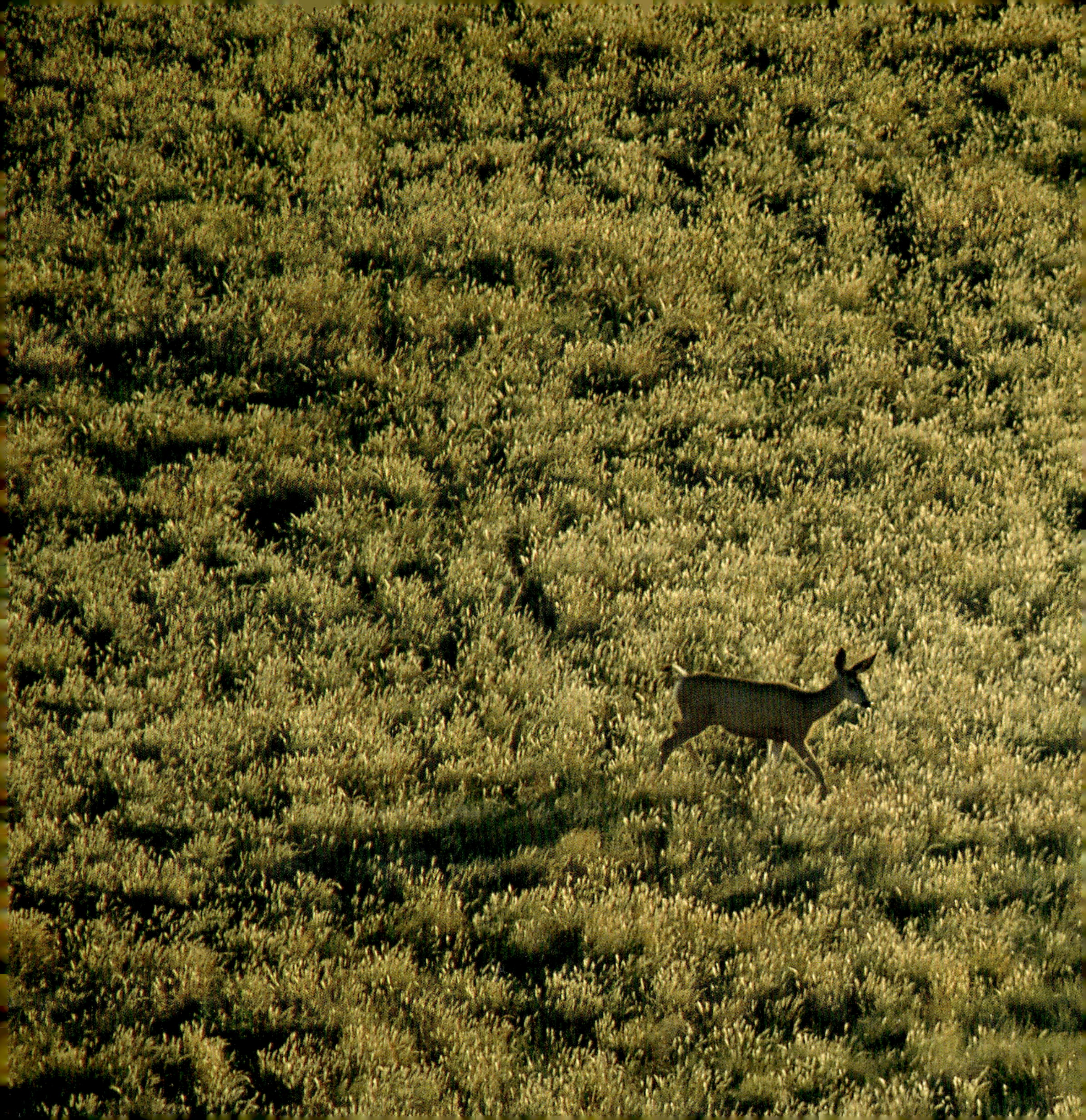

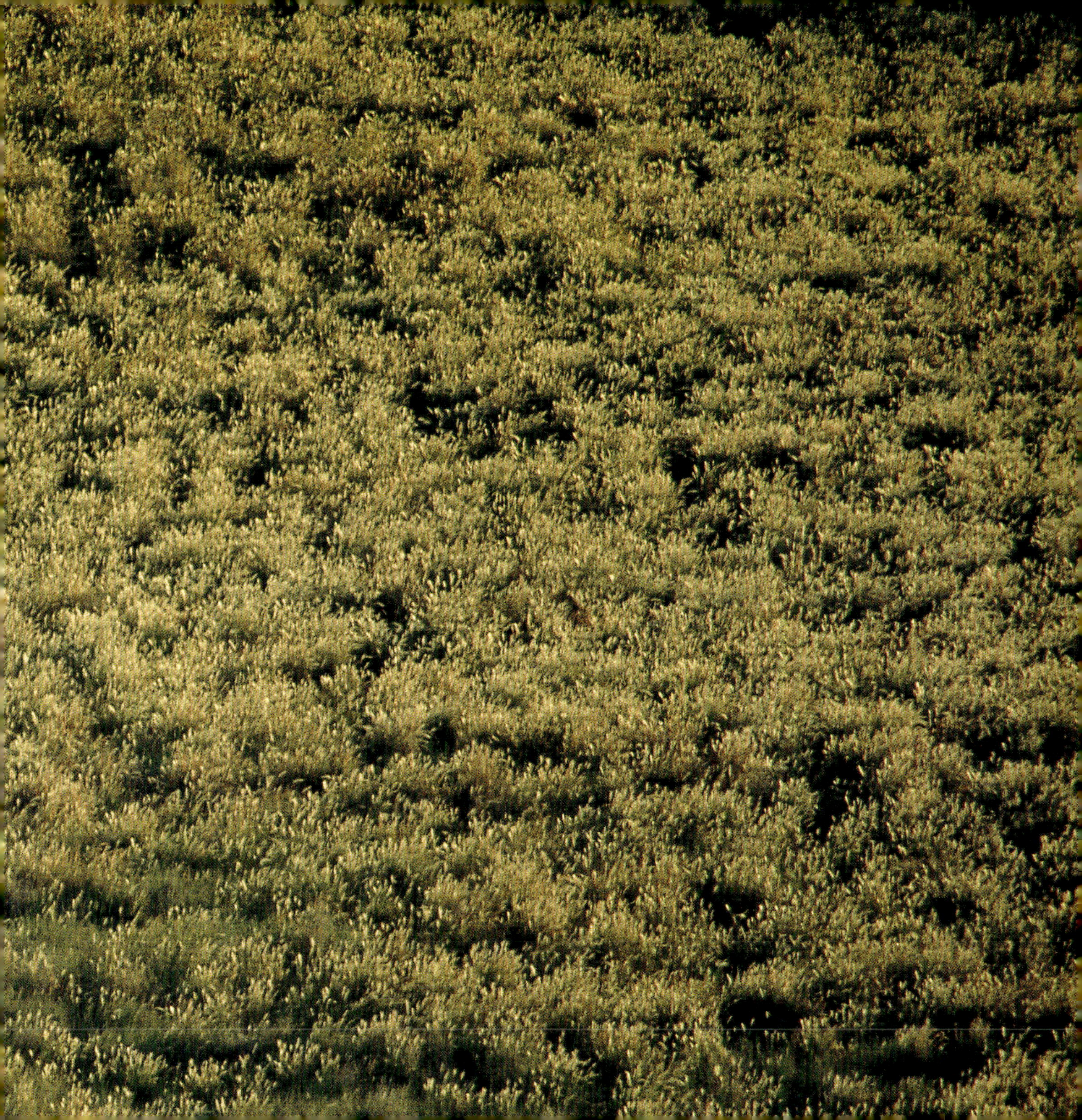

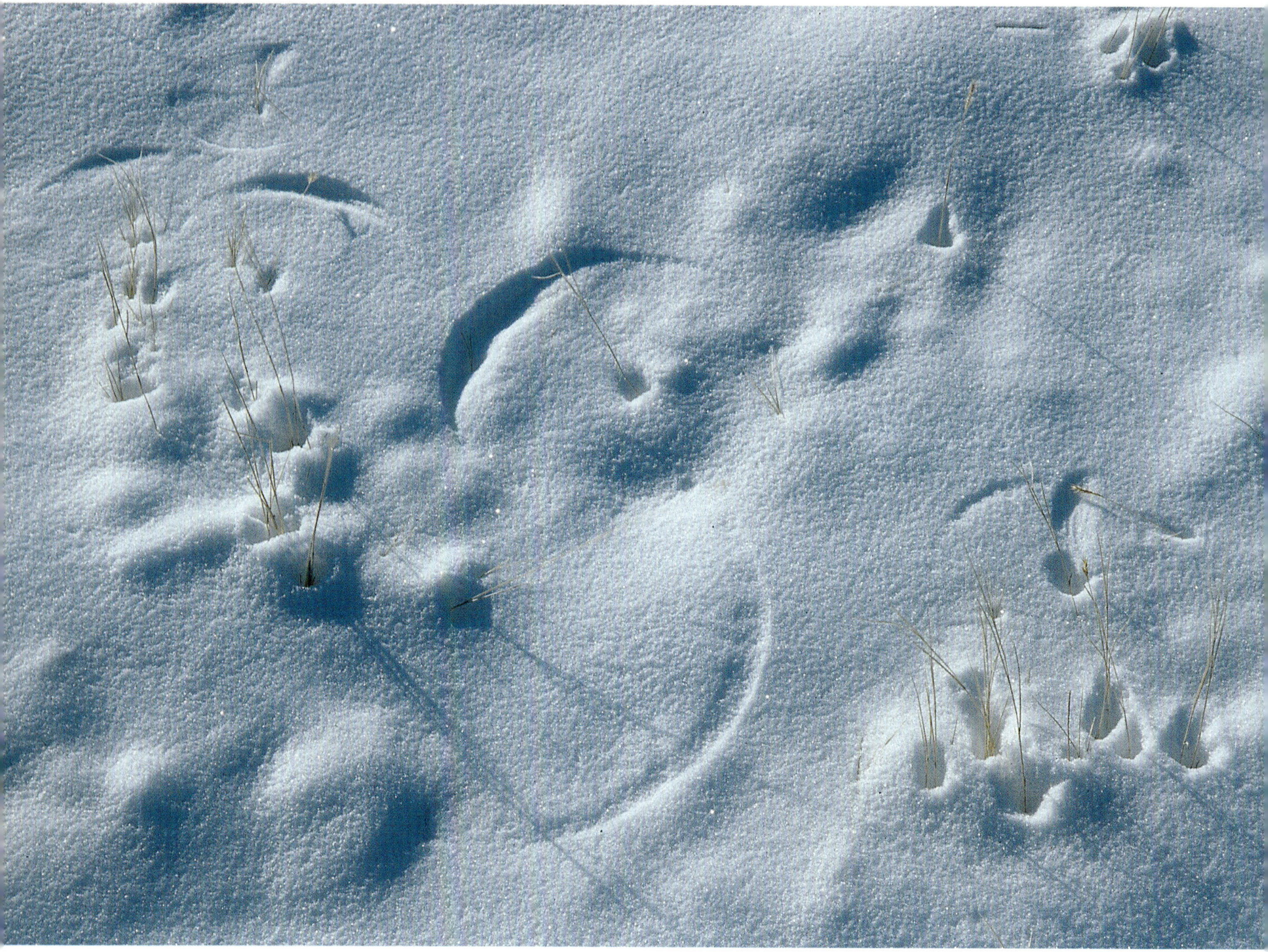

east side of the Cypress Hills, the plain slopes downward to the northeast and is broken by river valleys, coulees, and some uplands. The OMB is located within this area, on the eastern edge of the Old Man On His Back plateau.

Today, on this virtually treeless plain, the digger of a well or a dugout is sometimes startled to find a chunk of fossilized wood. About 12,000 years ago this treeless plain that is southern Saskatchewan was covered by a black spruce forest. But in the continuing, slow geologic movement (and to simplify a more complex process), as the air grew warmer, the land dried, and the forest retreated, until about 10,000 years ago, grassland appeared. At that time, or shortly after, this open prairie likely teemed with animal life: great herds of bison, numerous plains grizzly feeding on the elk, deer, and antelope, and the plains wolf running in packs freely through limitless fields of grass.

Originally, I found, almost a quarter of the earth's surface was grassland. It has even been suggested that hominids did not become humans until the formation of the African grasslands, when they came down out of the trees and learned, on the savannah, to walk upright.

Since the formation of the Great Plains, the changes to the appearance of what would become the OMB have been those caused by weather, by lightning-related fires, by the processes of steady wind pushing against thinly vegetated surfaces, and by water running between glacier-created hills, sometimes pooling to form sloughs, and sometimes digging into the earth, washing it away, until coulees are formed. ("Coulee," from the French *couler* meaning "to flow," is the term used for a channel down which melted snow and rainwater flow. Some coulees are very deep and wide, others only a few feet deep and so narrow that only a single human on a horse can ride through.) All other changes to the land are human-made: the draining of surface waters, or the damming of it; the gradual levelling by machinery of the once uneven surface, and the chopping down of any small outcroppings of trees; the extraction of oil, gas, and potash; and the greatest change of all—the modification and cultivation of the land for farming.

Even the grass makes angels in the snow.

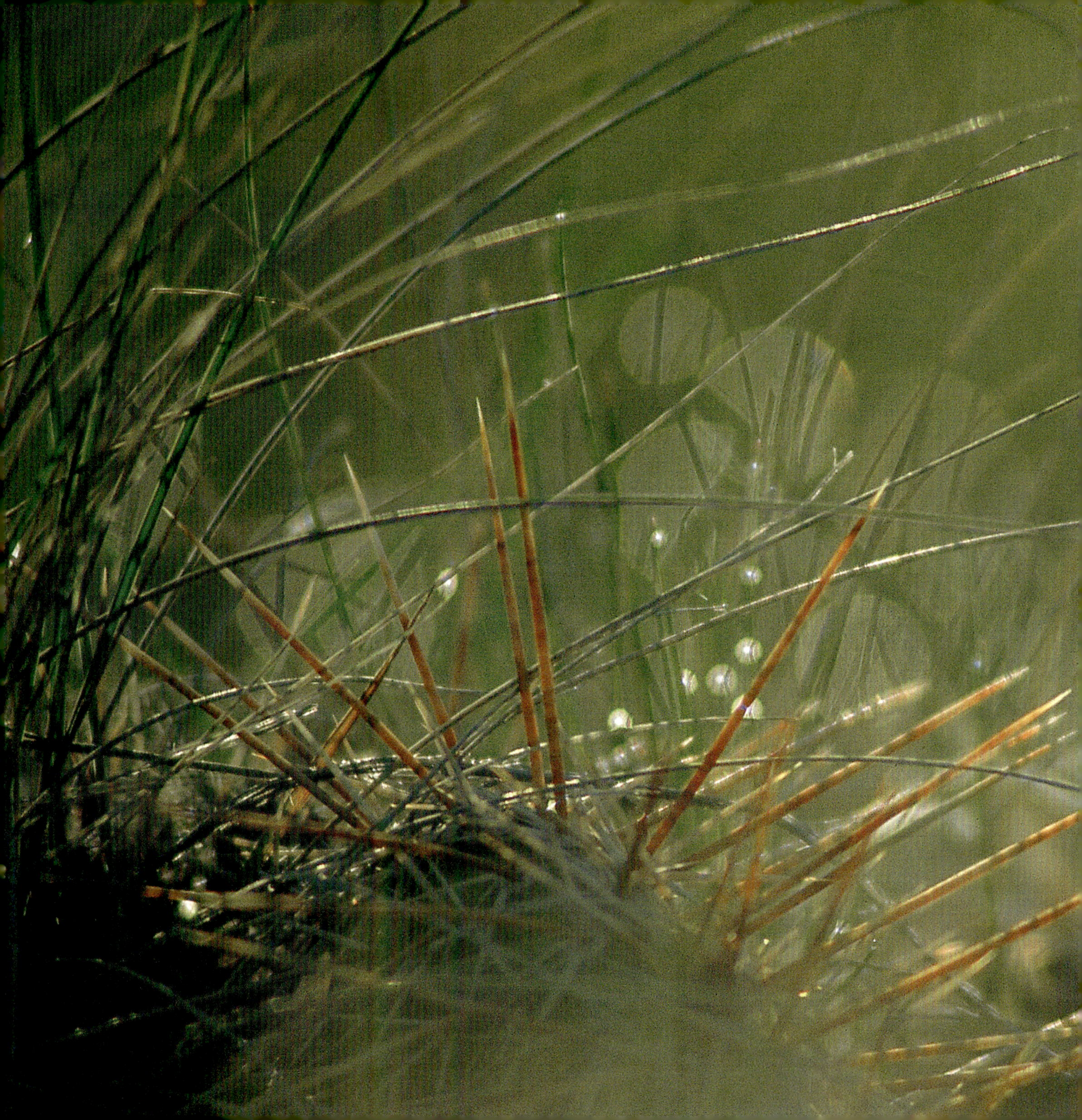

Unimaginably vast and powerful forces had acted to form the landscape I studied with such wonder when I first arrived here, even if it took me a long time to ask the question as to how it had become this way. As a child of the pioneering generation myself, although in the forested land far to the north, it was a while before I began to wonder who the first inhabitants of the land were. Like most Canadians of European background, I was satisfied to think that they had been our grandfathers and sometimes our great-grandfathers, that is, until I began my solitary walks.

Left: Prickly pear cactus hidden in the grass catches the walker unaware.

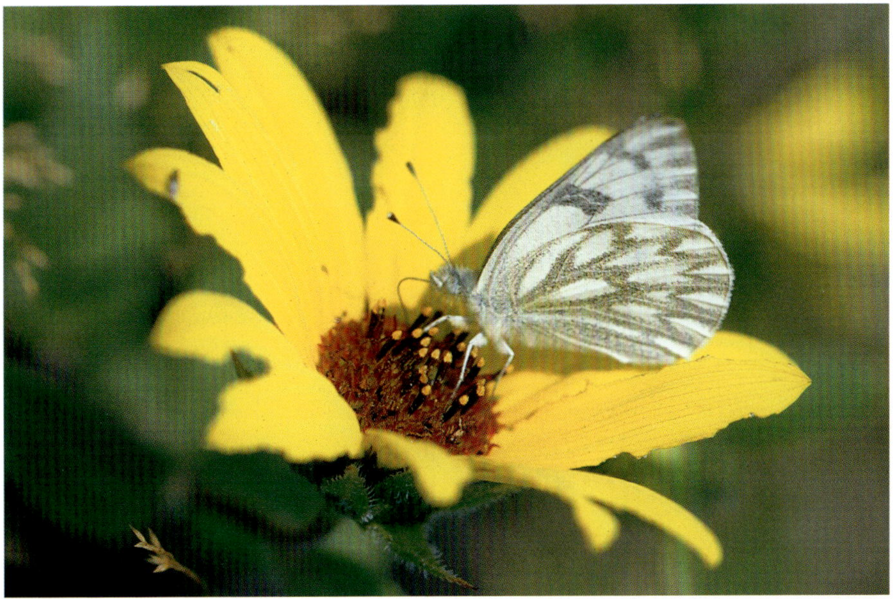

A burst of bright colour adds an accent to a pale landscape.

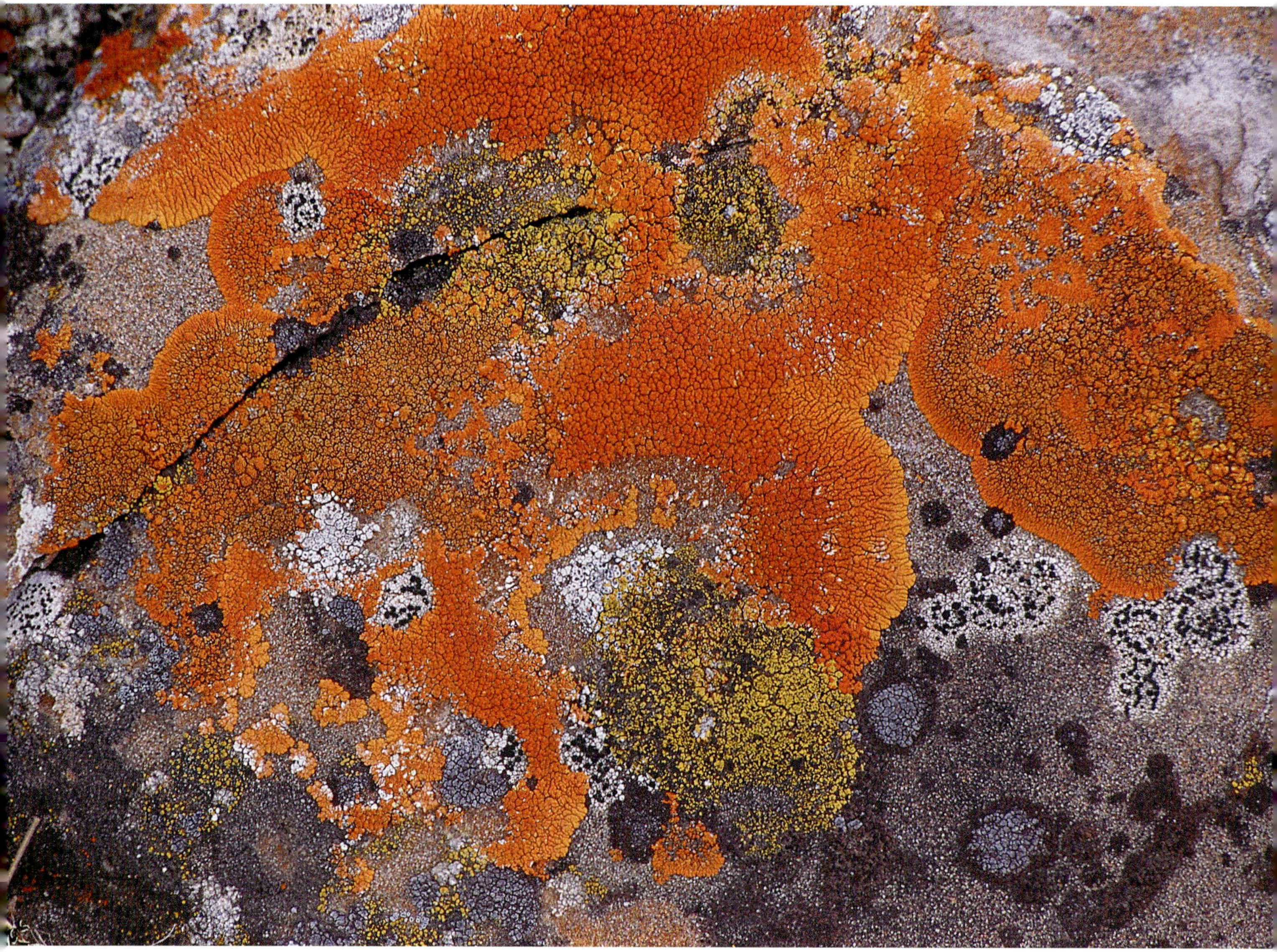

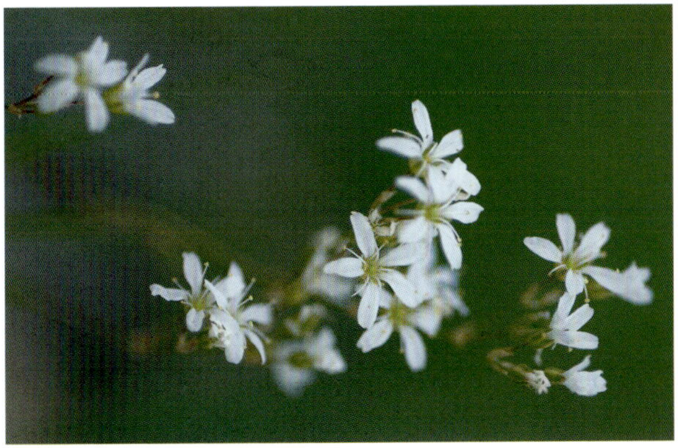

The First Inhabitants

Walking the prairie as I did, day after day, alone and thoughtful, I slowly began to notice what had always been there, though I had simply not seen them at first. These were stone circles, or other shapes made of stone lying in the grass, partially embedded in the ground, with blades of grass growing around and between them, and often partly covered with lichen in various colours, either brilliant rusts, gold, and greens, or paler shades of cream and grey. One day, early on in my years on the ranch—it was September, I think, and unusually hot—as I sat in the old ranch house, I began to be visited by an extreme and quite irrational desire to be outside walking on the prairie. I was trying to write, I remember, and this urge was so strong that I couldn't concentrate and finally, in exasperation, threw down my pen, grabbed my hat, and went out.

I remember that I walked rapidly straight east, as if I had an assignation and was hurrying to get there on time, although, in fact, I didn't have any plan in mind at all, and was all alone and knew that the chances I would meet someone out in the fields were about the same as winning a lottery. I remember also that I had a sense of urgency that grew stronger and

Left: The size and thickness of lichen is a clue to how long the ground has been undisturbed.

The rare and delicate rocky ground sandwort is common on the OMB.

stronger until I was half-running, until I crawled under a fence that took me into a part of what the Butalas have always called "the east field." Then my urgency transformed itself slowly into something more like a puzzling sense of having a destination, although I didn't know what the destination was, nor where.

But this force that so strangely gripped me took over and I found myself turning south, knowing this was the right way to go. I kept walking, climbing one high hill and staring south at the next one, knowing I was looking for something, although I did not know what it was I was looking for, only that I hadn't found it yet, so that I kept walking. I climbed another hill and saw a large rock in the distance, but when I reached it, I knew somehow that this wasn't what I was looking for. I climbed another hill, started down the far side, and there! That was the one! I knew as soon as I saw it that the large glacial erratic in the distance was my destination.

And now I was afraid. I couldn't have said what it was I was afraid of—all the grizzlies and wolves are long gone and coyotes almost never go near people, much less hurt them, and though there were range cattle in the field, they were just black dots in the distance—but I felt as though I were having to push back the air to keep walking. I struggled with myself, wanting one minute to turn and go straight back to the safety of home, and the next, urging myself not to be such a coward, but to follow this drive to wherever it might lead. In the end, I ran. I ran down the long slope, through the tall grass in the draw between hills, and up the other side, slowing as I drew nearer to a large dolomite rock, a buffalo rubbing stone, that sat near the low end of a long, gently sloping, fairly flat ridge.

I studied the rock for a few moments as this puzzling sense of urgency slowly subsided now that I had found the place I was meant to find. Then I began a slow meandering walk up the long, gentle slope, intending to go to its highest point, or from another angle, to the top of the hill. But as I walked I began to find stone formations in the grass, small circles, a few half-circles opened in different directions. These had always been here, but

Heavily grazed range reveals ancient Aboriginal stone circles.

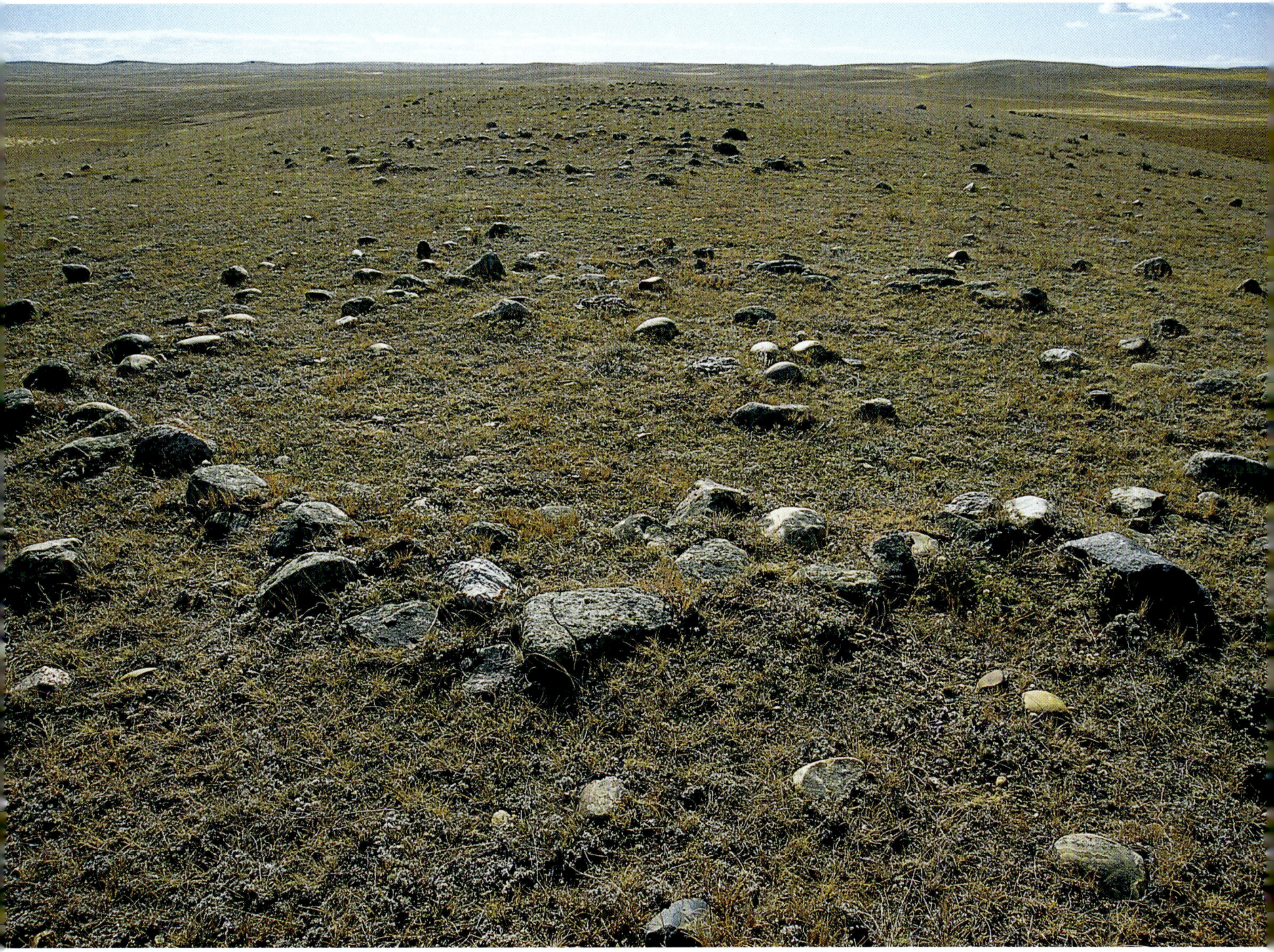

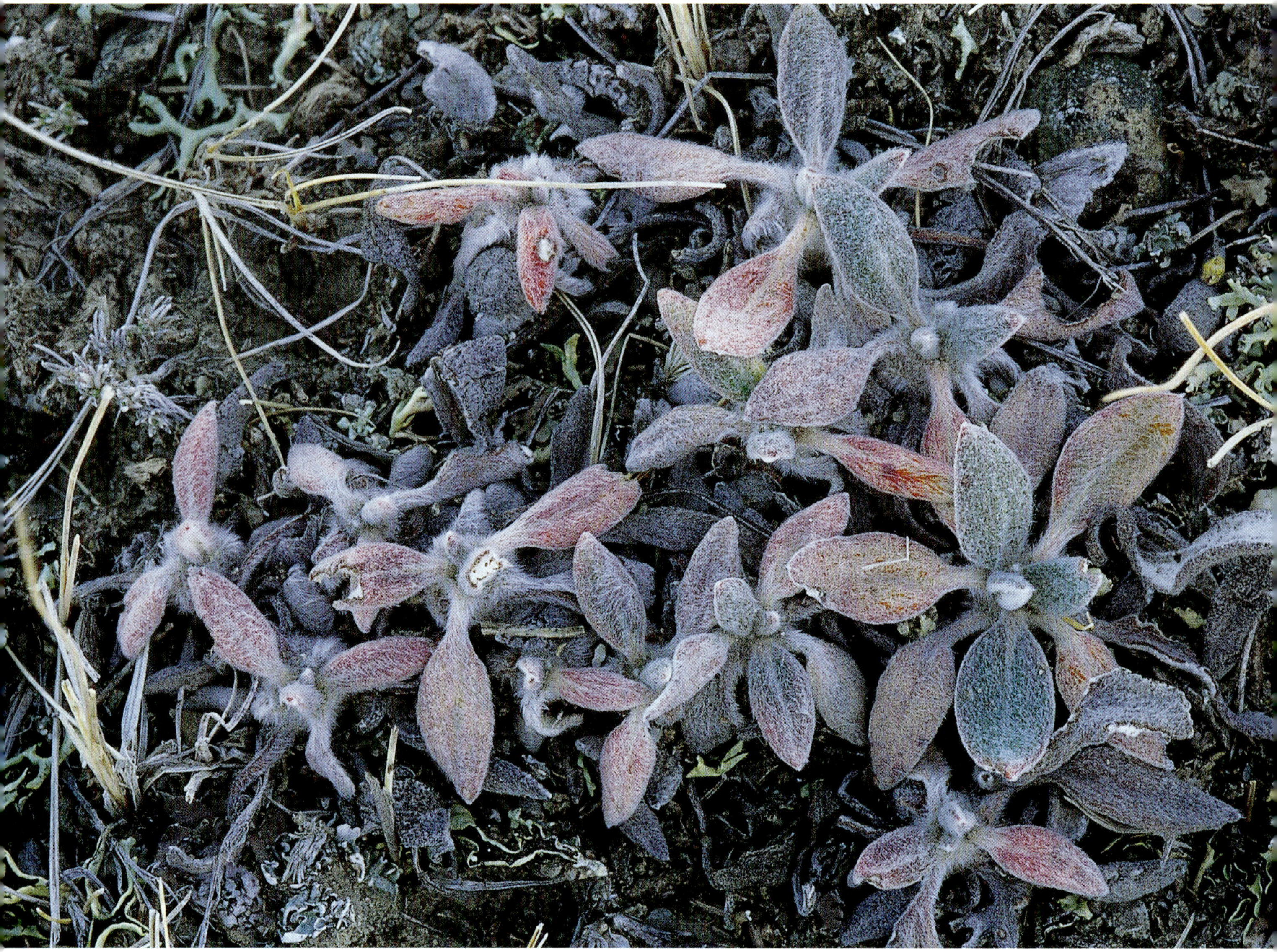

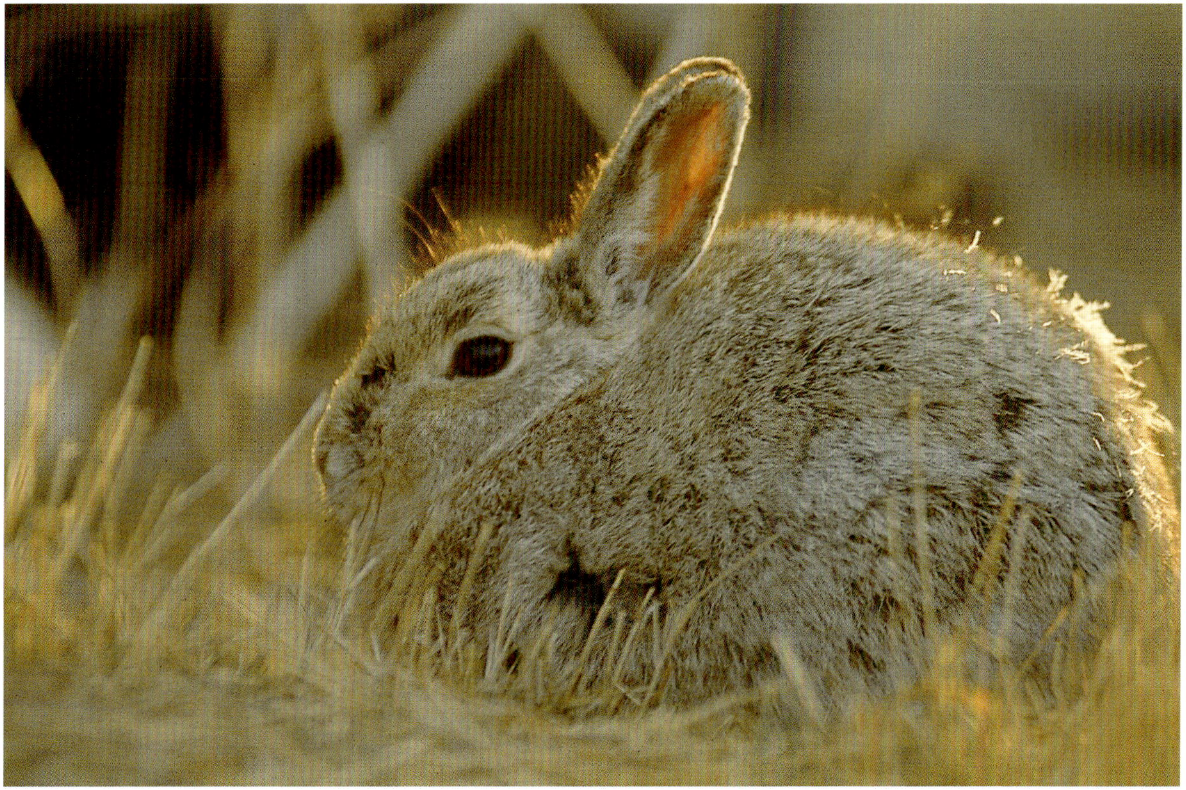

Another denizen native to this grassland is this little rabbit.

Left: One of the special beauties of grassland is the subtlety of its colouring.

I'd never noticed them, and now that I did, I was awestruck, walking with bated breath, my heart clenched in my chest. One after the other I found them until I came to a certain circle just big enough for me to lie down in. Carefully, I stepped into it. What had just happened to me, what I was now finding, seemed to me almost miraculous: I was filled with a sense of something I thought must be holy, and I felt a need for an expression of this, a need to perform homage to whatever it was that had brought me out here.

I stepped into the circle; I felt a need to be close to the earth and so I sat down, my legs extended in front of me, and I waited. Nothing. Still I had this feeling of a presence leading me. I stood then, the ever-present wind ruffling my hair, the sun warming my face and hands, and, not knowing what else to do to express my awe and my gratitude, I turned slowly and paused as I faced each of the four directions.

This was the first of many amazing experiences I was to have in nature, which I group, for want of a better name, under the heading of *spiritual.* Through these experiences I began to develop the strongest respect for nature—whatever nature might turn out to be. And new questions arose: *Who had made the stone circles and when?* If I knew this, then maybe the answers to the larger questions would follow.

We don't know when humans first came to the northern part of the Great Plains, but it is thought that the human history of the OMB area begins with the retreat of the ice of the Wisconsin glaciation beginning around 14,000 years ago. The oldest dated sites of human habitation in Saskatchewan found so far are, in fact, in the southwest part of the province at the Niska site near Ponteix, 72 miles northeast of the OMB, and the Heron Eden site, about 100 miles north, where artifacts have been dated to between 8,000 and 9,000 years ago. It seems reasonable to suppose that at the same time people were also occupying the nearby OMB area.

An archaeological survey of the OMB has not yet been completed, but as I walked over its undisturbed areas—most of its more than 13,000 acres—it was evident to me from the stone circles and cairns I was finding that people had been here before the Europeans, had lived and hunted here, and had known the place well. Many of the formations had been disturbed by weather, animals, and humans, but others remained complete, as nearly as I was able to tell, just as they were laid at an undetermined time in the past.

Before the first settlers came, I was told, there had been also stone tools on the prairie—hide-scrapers, hammers, awls—and also stone arrowheads and spearpoints. As none of these features or artifacts have been dated, and in the absence so far of projectile points (which can often be identified as belonging to known periods), who the builders of the stone circles and cairns were, or when during the last 10,000 or more years they built them,

Saskatchewan's native pronghorns are a different species from the better-known African antelope.

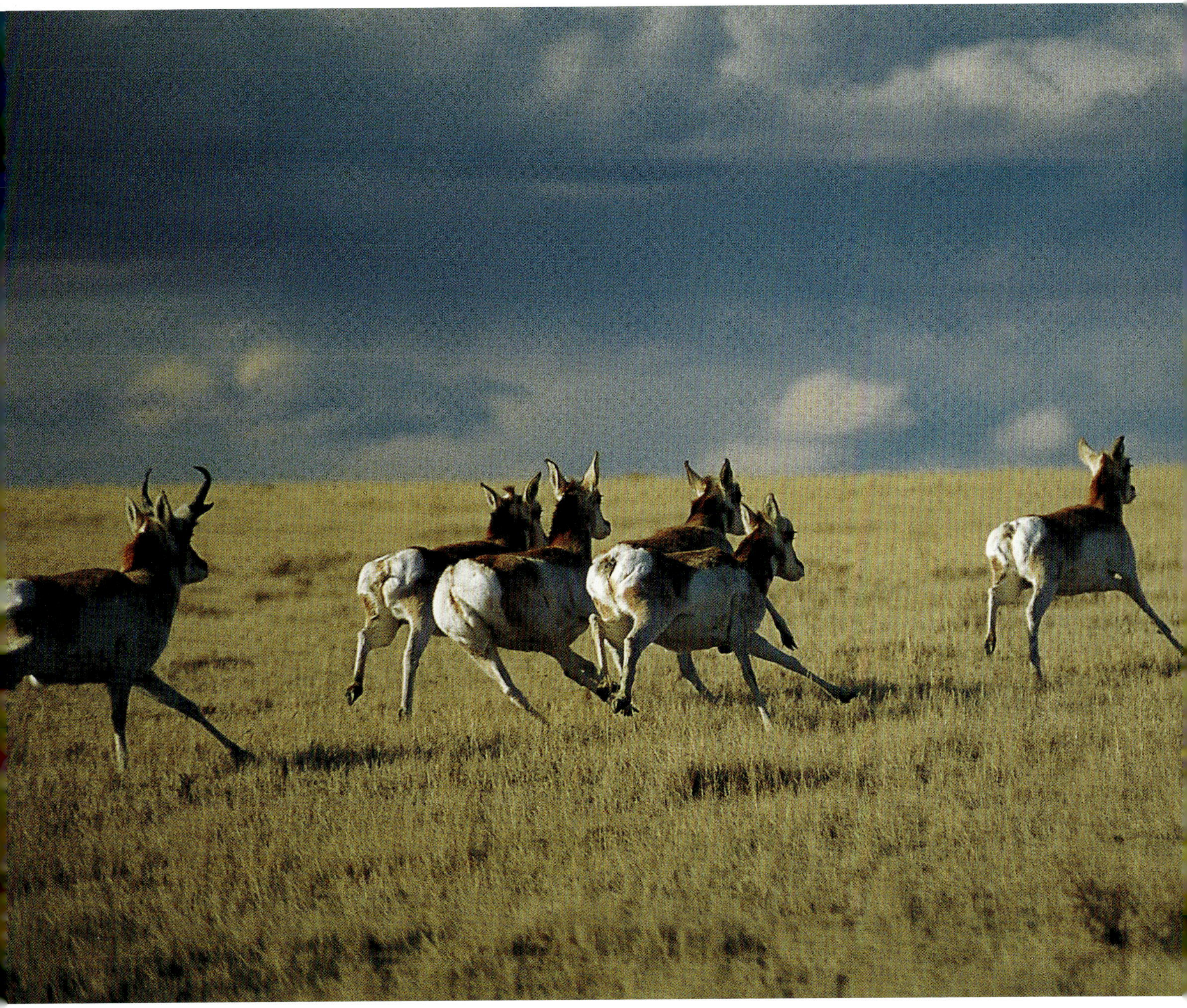

isn't known. But these were the artifacts of people who were, of course, hunter-gatherers rather than agriculturalists.

Much of their long history since the melting of the ice is unknown, but we know who the people were just before the arrival of the first Europeans and after. The Shoshone were known to have passed through the area, and the Gros Ventre, and probably in most recent times, the Siksika, the Nakota, the Plains Cree, and in the 1870s, some Lakota.

Conditions varied across the centuries, but in recent times, by midsummer on the OMB, surface water, except for one spring, would be in short supply, and since there are no trees, there would be no wood for fire, nor is there much natural shelter from bad weather on the OMB—only one moderately deep coulee and no trees—and fierce winds sweep around the hills without obstruction. Common sense would suggest that, at least in winter, the people would go elsewhere. A traveller, noting these conditions, might pause to wonder why people would camp there at all, but the reason is, of course, to hunt the vast herds of bison, ice age animals that roamed the area and whose bodies were the basis of the Plains peoples' culture, providing most of the food supply, clothing, shelter, and spiritual inspiration. It has been estimated that at their peak there were between 50 and 60 million bison roaming the grasslands, yet humans—both Europeans and Aboriginal people—managed to extirpate them from the northern Great Plains by the end of the 1870s.

I had been led out of my house that unseasonably hot September day as forcefully as if I'd been taken by the hand, until I'd found those remnants of the bison-hunting culture—the stone circles. The experience left me with a strong sense of a presence out there on the land, something powerful, something full of will and desire. But I did not know what it was.

I tried, as always, to find explanations in books. Reading the words of Plains people as quoted, and then as they wrote them themselves, I slowly gained a small degree of understanding of their worldview, which was deeply bound up with, and inseparable from, the nature in which they lived.

Much of the non-meat diet of some Aboriginal groups was provided by this plant, silverleaf psoralea, *and its sister plant, called Indian breadroot.*

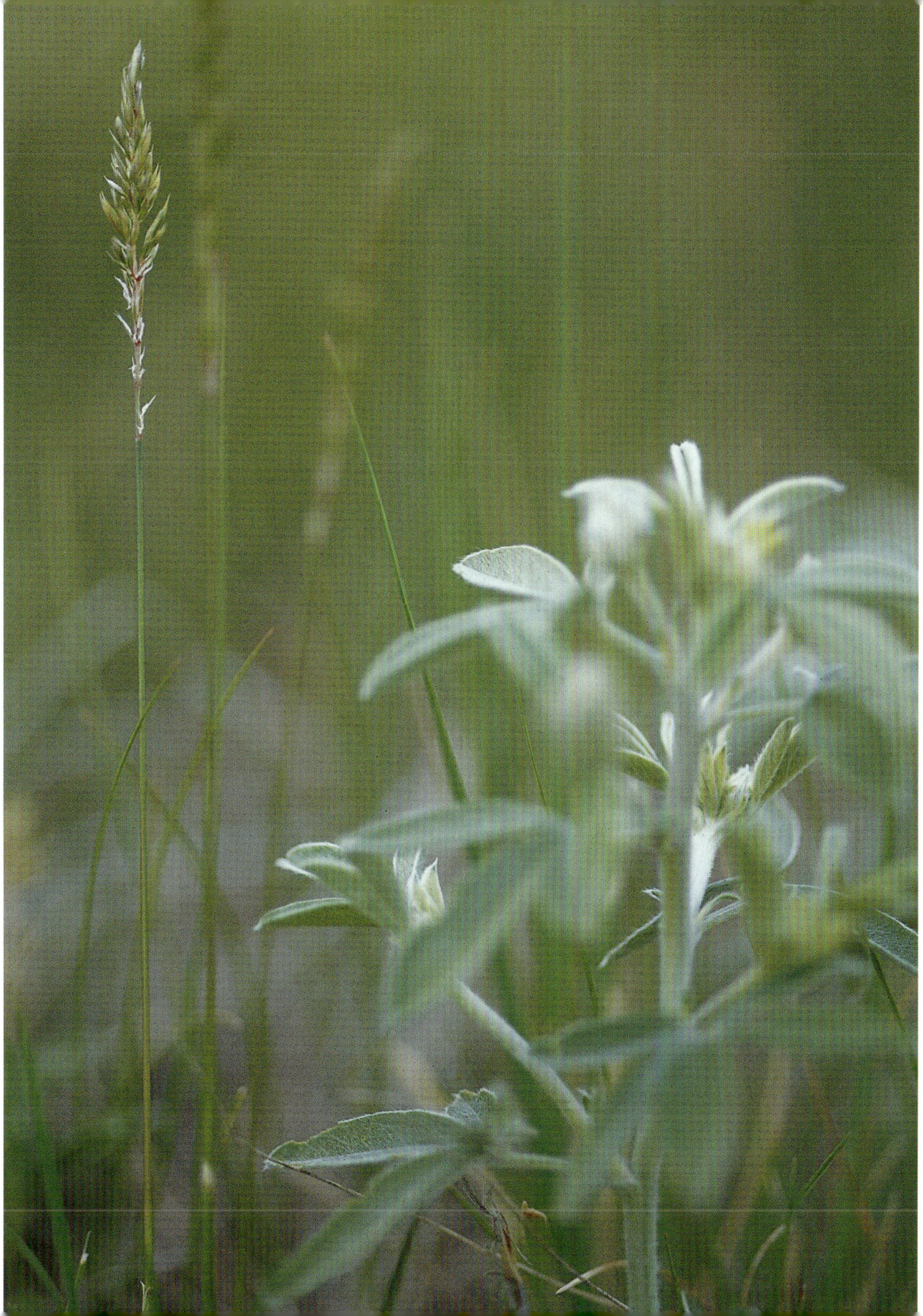

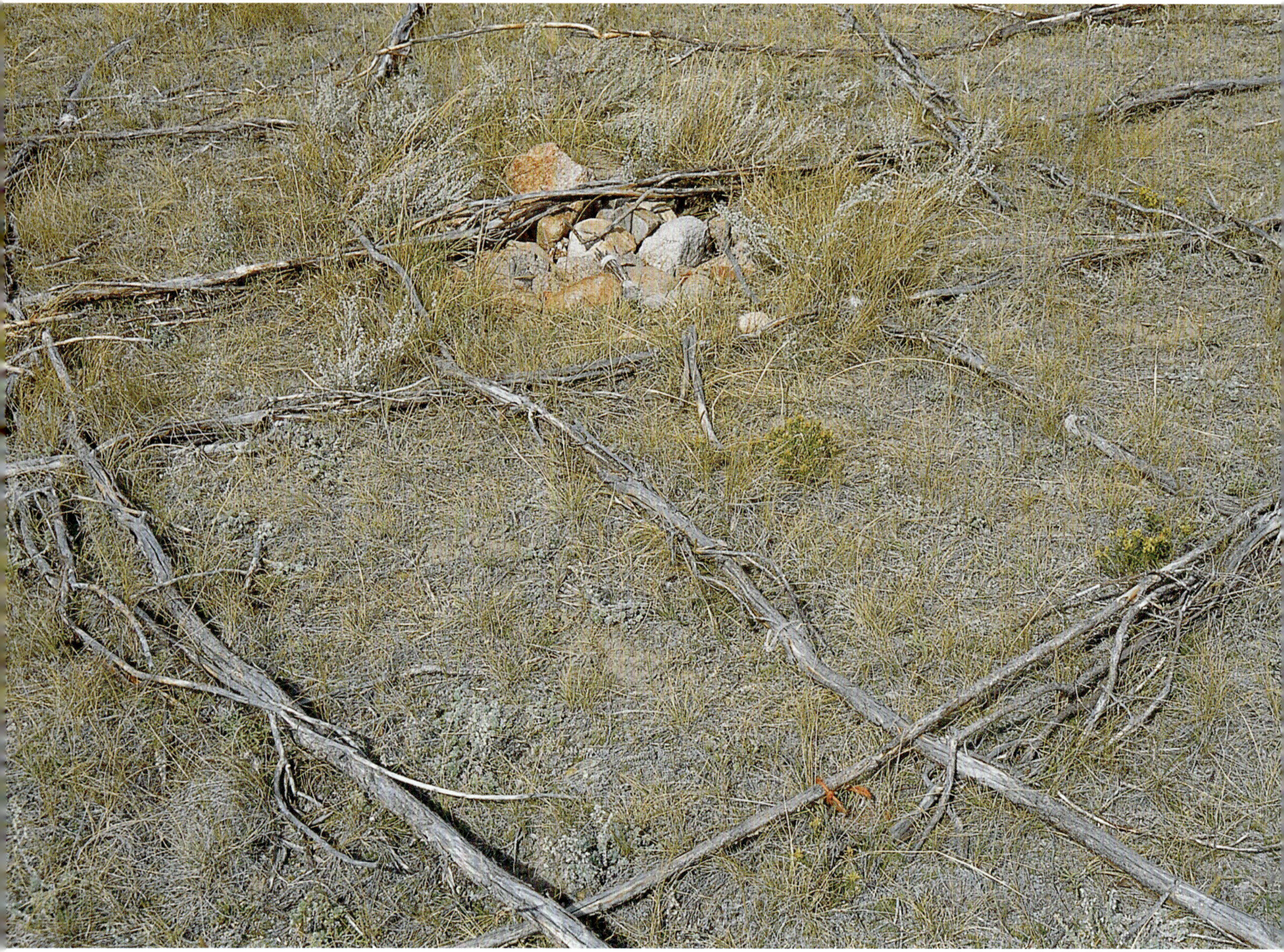

Basic to this worldview is a hierarchy of being that, as with Christianity, has at the top the Creator, but just below the Creator is Mother Earth, not human beings as in the Christian belief. Below Mother Earth come the Sun, Plants, the Moon and Stars, followed by Small Life, then by the Winged and Aquatic, then by Two-and-Four-Legged Animals, and, last, by Human Beings. Surprising and unacceptable as it is to most Christians, such a belief system, nonetheless, requires of the human race a profound humility toward, and a deep reverence for, all other aspects of nature.

I found also that the four directions as well as the sky and the earth were each considered to have their own spirits and that worship involved saying prayers to each of these six directions—or as nearly as I could understand, or could read between the lines of what I found. And then, with a shock, I remembered back to the day that September when a mysterious power or presence had led me out onto the land and shown me that it had been inhabited before by a people who had a strong spiritual life, and that power had guided me gently to face each of the four directions as a way of honouring the presence I had just made contact with.

This belief system also precluded the private ownership of land. For many generations, Aboriginal people had used the land communally, although within this communal system they had also had territories primarily used by one group or another. And yet, after many centuries of living on the land, these people had apparently vanished. There weren't any native people on the streets of the town, or anywhere about. I had spent nearly all my life in Saskatchewan, and wherever I had lived in the province, they had always been there, in the background, on the periphery of non-Aboriginal society. Now to see none at all (and not knowing the reason for this) puzzled me.

The willow frame of the ceremonial sweatlodge, part of inauguration ceremonies for the OMB, has been laid to rest on the prairie.

When I asked the local people where the native people had gone, they seemed not to have given their disappearance that much thought, accepting it, I suppose, as natural and right. I began to search the literature to find out what had happened to them. The answer, I found, lay in history.

The "Company of Adventurers of England Trading into Hudson's Bay" was given a royal charter in 1670 to all the area drained by streams that ran into that bay. This area, the northwest of the continent, was called Rupert's Land, after Prince Rupert, the company's first governor and the veritable emperor of a fur empire so vast that no one even knew its precise boundaries. The company ruled it for two hundred years, during that time subverting many of the Aboriginal people from their original way of life—they had lived, ideally, under a dictum not to take any more animals than necessary for their own needs—and introducing them to alcohol and to the devastation wrought by European diseases such as smallpox. In 1870, the Hudson's Bay Company sold its charter (for £300,000 plus about 6.6 million acres of land) to the new Canadian government which renamed the area the North-West Territories, and this government began the process of further subjugating the First Nations people.

In the early 1880s, with the bison gone from the prairie, the Aboriginal people, starving now, moved into the Cypress Hills to the North West Mounted Police's headquarters at Fort Walsh, where they hoped to obtain food. The governor at the time, Edgar Dewdney, determined to clear all southwestern Saskatchewan of First Nations people, refused them food unless they "took treaty" and agreed to move to reserves set out for them north of the South Saskatchewan River or east of Regina.

Seeing no other choice, eventually all but a leader called Nekaneet and his few followers did as was required of them, and left. The result is that the only native reserve today in the area bounded by the Alberta and Montana borders, the South Saskatchewan River, and the few Dakota people east at Wood Mountain, is the Nekaneet reserve. It sits in the Cypress Hills about 50 miles north of the OMB and is occupied chiefly by Cree people. (The Nakota people of the Carry the Kettle reserve also came originally from the Cypress Hills area.) Now I knew, despite the remnants of their civilization everywhere the prairie hadn't been ploughed, why there were no people left. Their removal left the area open for Europeans to move in.

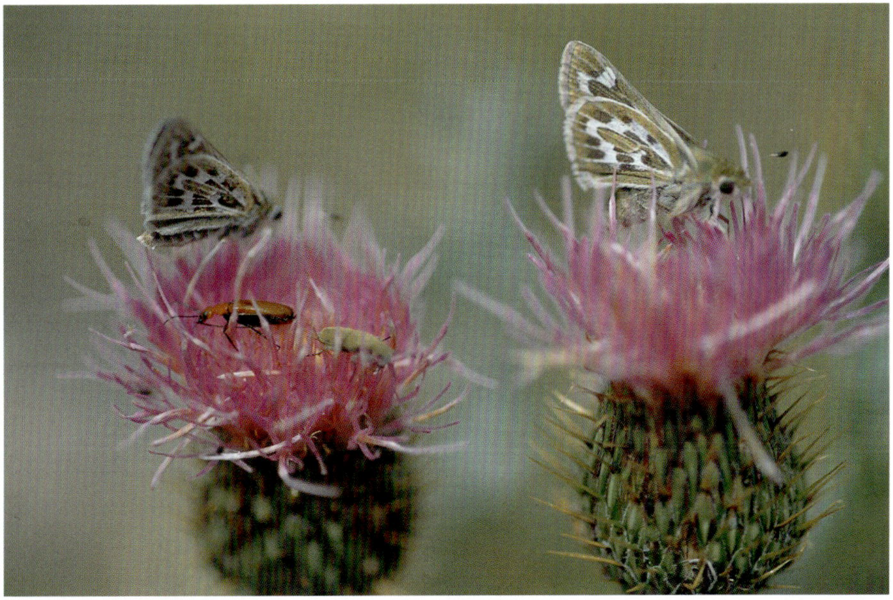

On close inspection, the prairie teems with life.

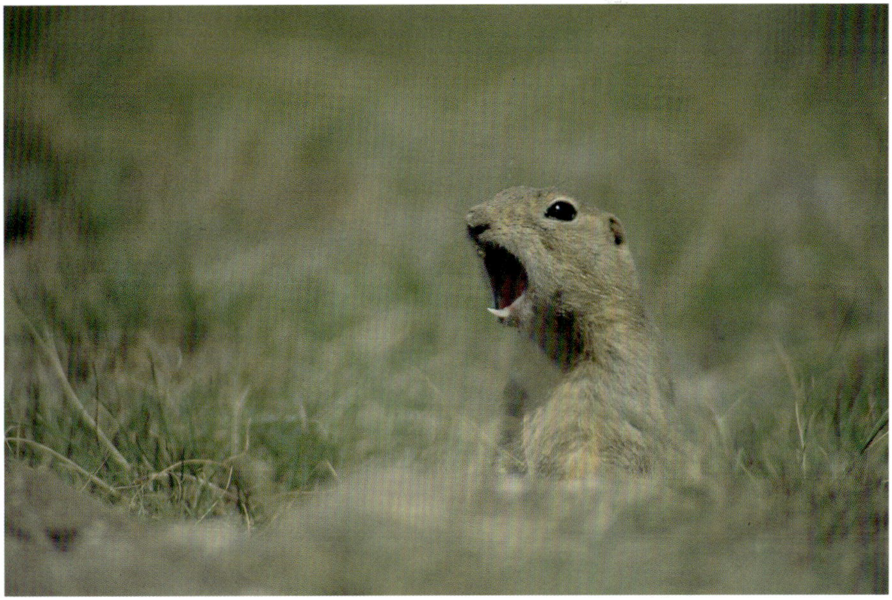

This Richardson ground squirrel, or gopher, projects a ferocity that belies its small size.

Following pages: The classic prairie landscape of earth and sky.

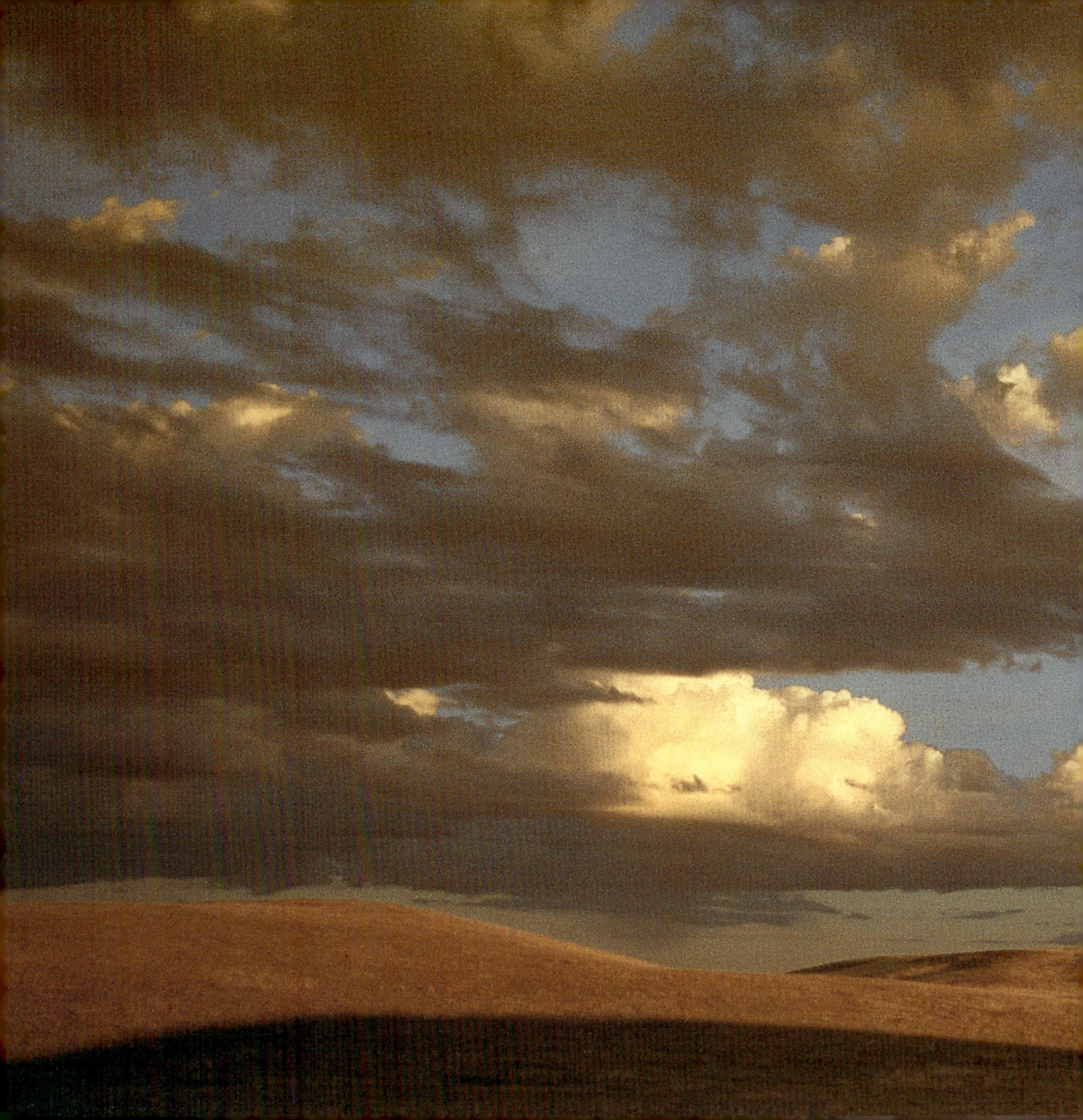

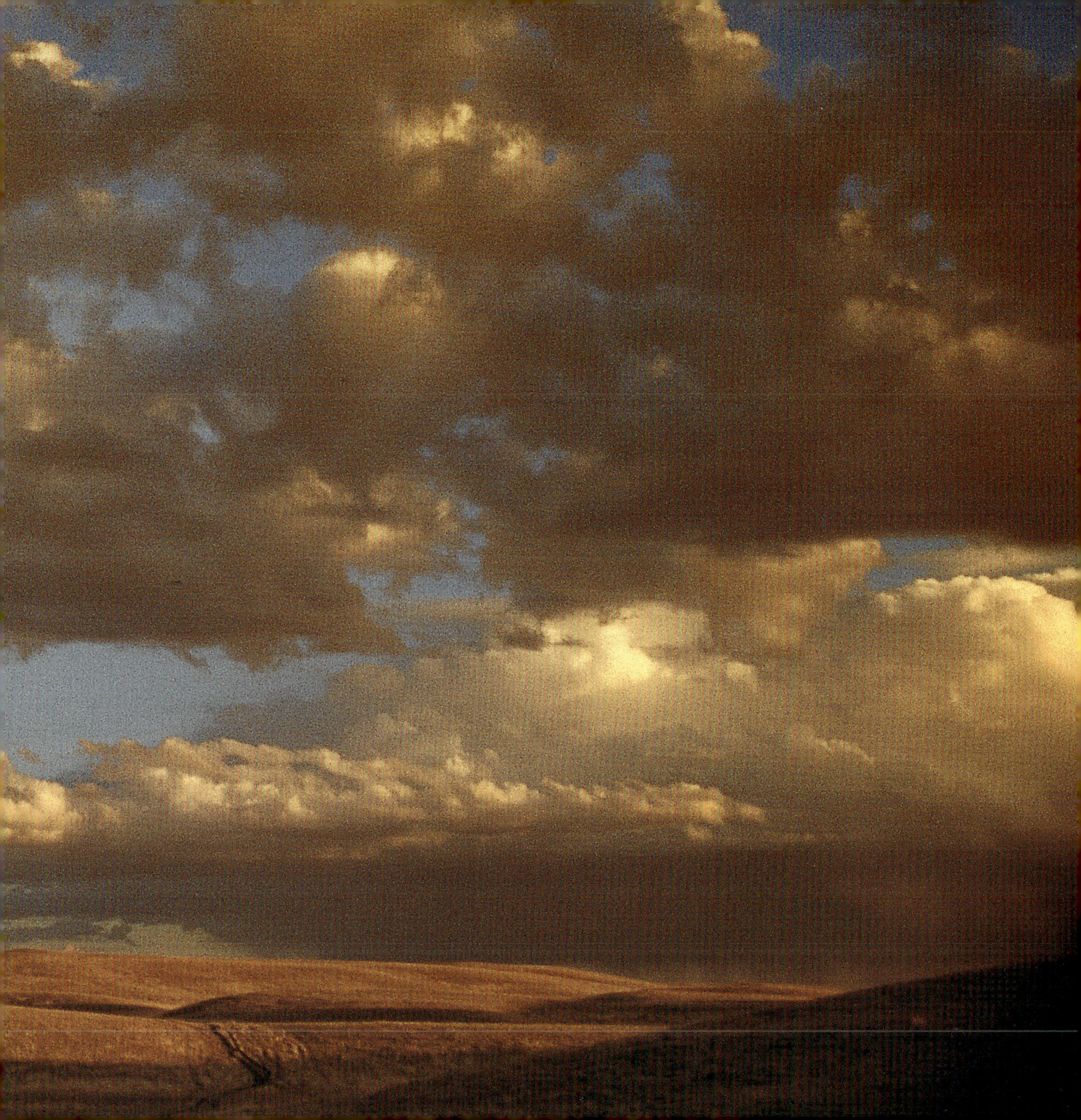

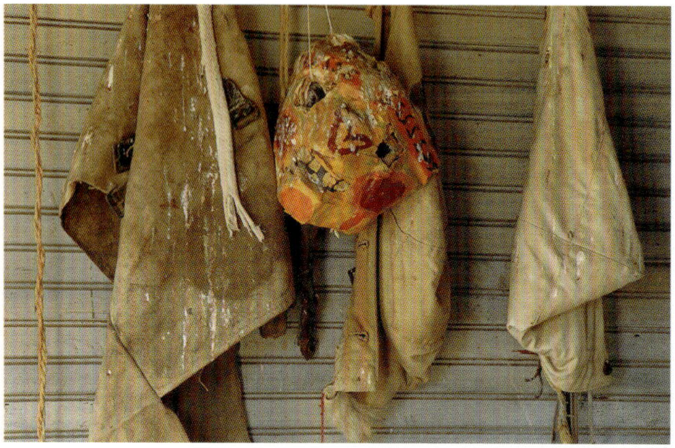

The Ranching Life

After the extirpation of the bison and the subduing and removing of the Aboriginal nations, the Canadian range was opened to ranching. This occurred at the same time as the opening of the eastern plains of Montana, and cattle flowed into the Canadian prairies from the east and the south, their owners looking for cheap (or free) grazing land still in good condition. The formation of enormous ranches became possible when in late 1881 the Canadian government allowed the leasing of up to 100,000 acres of grazing land per rancher, for up to twenty-one years, at the low rate of 1 cent per acre or, at the most, $1,000 per year. Not surprisingly, a large and profitable cattle industry centred in Calgary, Alberta, developed.

As early as 1888, large areas of what is today southwestern Saskatchewan were part of grazing leases that extended from ranch headquarters in Alberta district into Assiniboia district (the names of the districts within the North-West Territories). The OMB was likely part of the huge lease of the Empire Cattle Company whose headquarters in 1906 were near Willow Creek, and possibly of the T Bar Down whose headquarters were south of Eastend.

Settlers' artifacts remind us touchingly of the human cost of breaking the prairie.

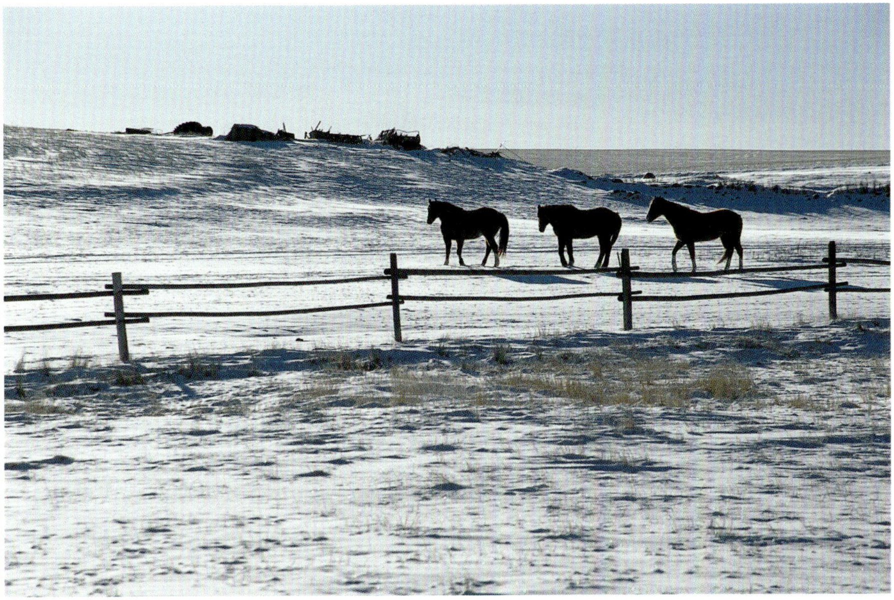

Horses first arrived on the northern Great Plains in the eighteenth century.

With the arrival of ranchers, a new view of land took precedence, some aspects of which continue among old-fashioned ranchers to this day: they considered themselves not only as potential owners, but also as "stewards" or managers of nature. In the early days, though, most of the ranchers didn't own much land, but instead rented it. The leases often covered so much territory that the land would be grazed by more than one rancher's cattle without it seeming to cause much trouble.

A rancher's kingdom has always been made of grass, and, ideally, he will treasure it, think it beautiful, do his best to "save" fields of it for the times when he will need it for his cattle. It is also very much in his interests to move the cattle before they graze a field too thoroughly, weakening the plants' roots and thus allowing invaders such as sage, cactus, cinquefoil, and greasewood (none of which cattle make use of, although antelope do) to fill in wide areas that would otherwise be grass. As well, a traditional rancher is proud of his expert knowledge about the plants in his fields and

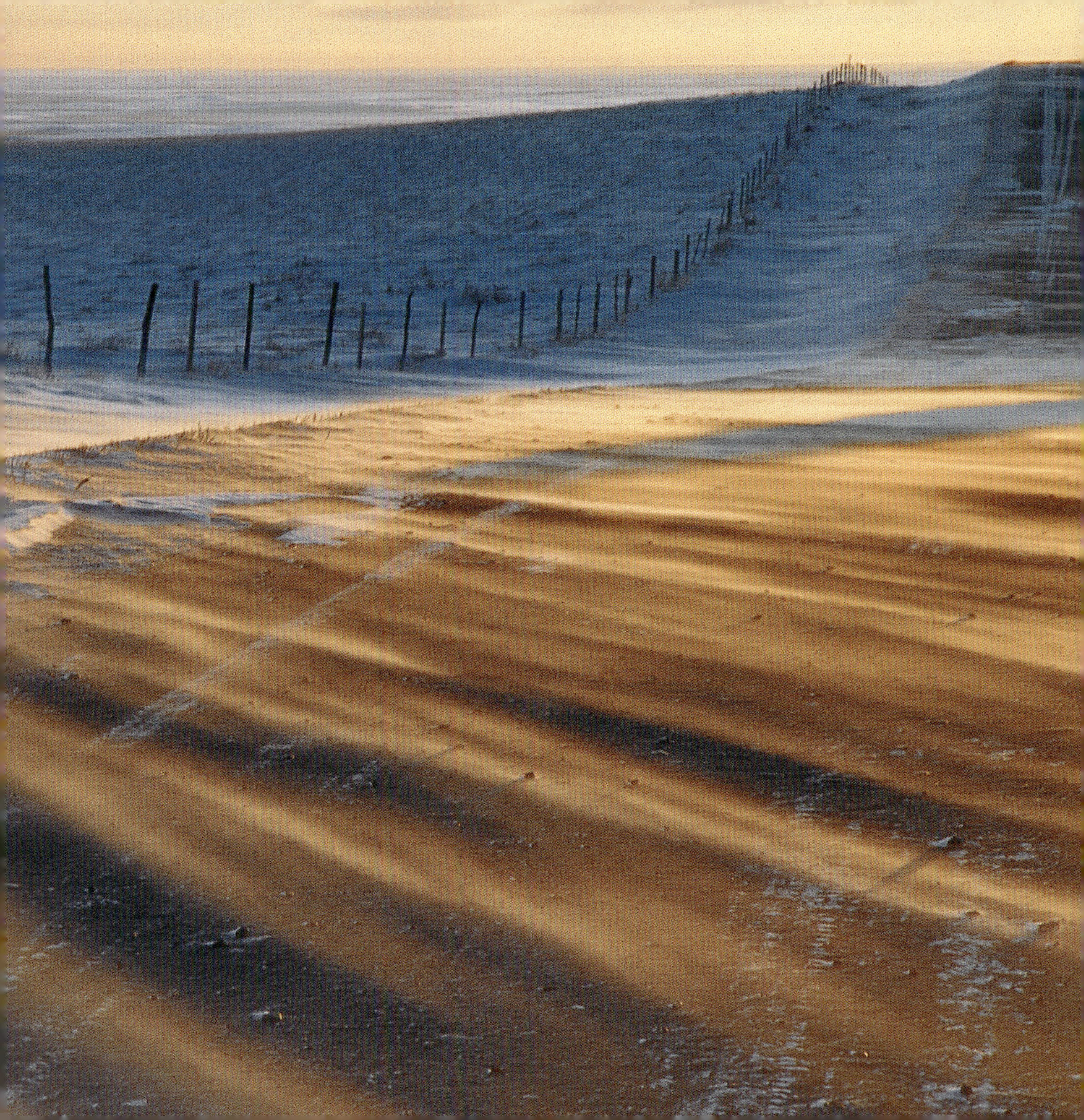

their condition at any moment. What matters to him about grass is the nutritiousness of each variety of plant and when it is at its peak in nutrient value, as well as the preferences of cattle—what they will eat, and when, and what they will not eat. A rancher's assessment of a field of grass will include the "cover," that is, how thick and tall the grass is, and the proportion of non-edible plants, such as sage, cactus, and greasewood, to edible plants.

It was Peter who taught me all this, as we rode day after day moving the cattle from one field to another, chasing home a sick one to be doctored, cutting out the steers to be sold, bringing in the bulls or spreading them out among the herd in the spring, and working in the corral with the men sorting cattle or, in some peripheral way, helping with brandings and the "mothering up" afterwards. Cattle ranching was indeed a business to him, a way to make a living, and he followed the markets as closely as anyone and kept up with the latest information in farm and ranch newspapers and magazines.

But he taught me too that the rancher also takes great pride in the "wildness" of his land, seeing himself as the first real conservationist, and tries to keep it as wild as possible by not ploughing and seeding it to introduced grasses such as Crested wheat or Russian wild rye, or by not driving out the native animals that inhabit it. His attitude toward land use is that he can graze cattle on it, making a living for himself and his family, and still maintain its beauty and wildness, which, for him, is the best reason to be a rancher in the first place.

Charles, John, and George Butala, natives of Slovakia, arrived at what eventually became their family ranch in 1913, although John and Charles had been in North Amerca since 1904. They each applied, under the Dominion Lands Act, for 160 acres of land, John's and Charles's adjacent to each other, George's on the next section. Over the years they slowly acquired more land as, one by one, the smallholders left, either abandoning their homesteads or, if they owned them, selling them. Either through purchase or lease, by 1977, when Peter's father George died—John had died in the sixties and Charles

Although there is little snow, nearly every winter brings a few days of cold as extreme as 50 degrees below Fahrenheit.

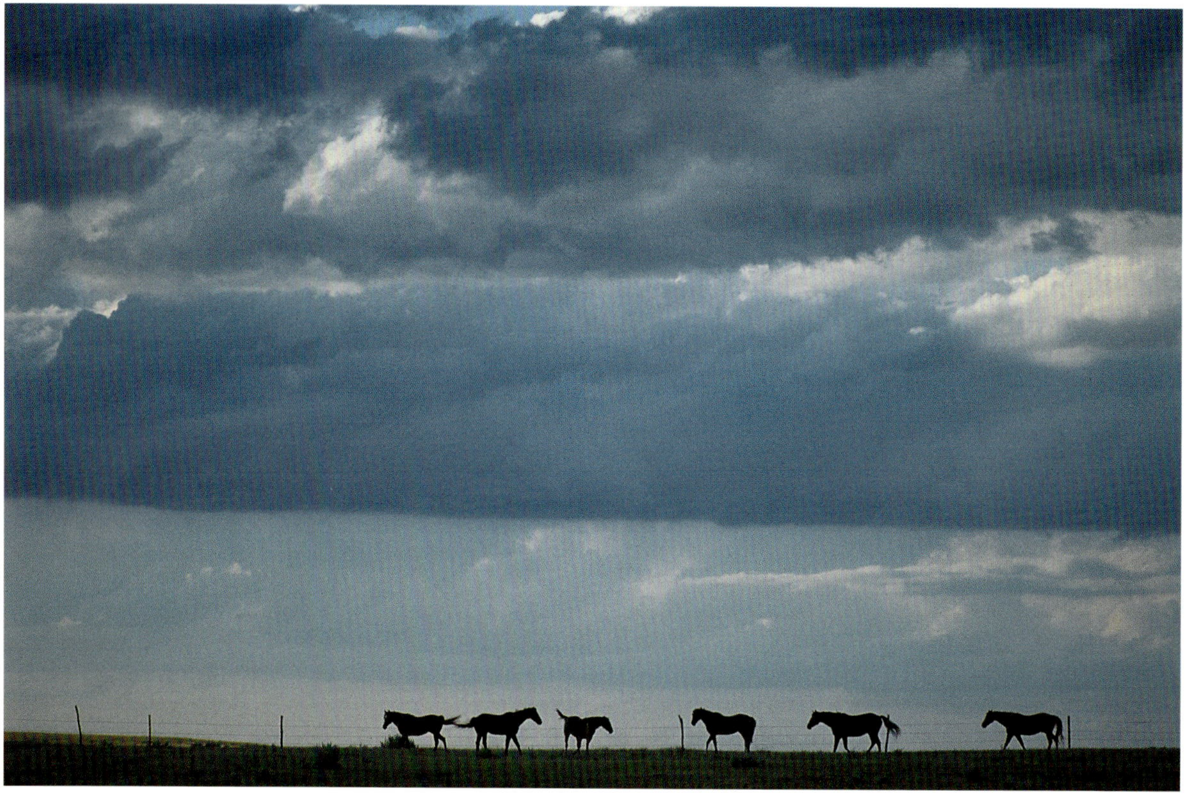

Horses at play on the prairie.

in the seventies—the Butalas held about 10,000 acres in 21-to-33-year leases from the provincial government, and owned about 3,000 acres, all of this, happily, in one large block. Although the Butala brothers had ploughed some land for crop as was required under the act, for the most part, they preferred to leave the grass as it was and to raise cattle on it. This was the then-growing cattle ranch to which George's wife, the young teacher Alice Graham, who was born on a farm in Manitoba established in 1885, came in the early thirties. It was the ranch on which Peter and his two younger sisters, Mary Jane and Nancy, were raised, and which, with his father's death, became Peter's; this was the vast acreage of stunningly beautiful grassland to which I came in 1976.

To know the OMB as a rancher knows it, the traveller will have to stop gazing upward at the clouds and look downward to his feet, for what looks to a stranger like wide fields of undifferentiated grass is instead an abundance of plants: grasses yes, but also sedges, forbs, shrubs, more than two hundred kinds of plants in all, some of them as commonplace as—well—grass, others of varying degrees of rarity.

This is one of a number of wheat grasses native to the mixed-grass prairie.

There are three categories of grassland: tall-grass prairie, mixed-grass prairie, and short-grass prairie. The OMB falls into the mixed-grass category where the most characteristic and abundant grasses are classified as mid-height, such as the wheat grasses—northern and western—and needle grasses—green and needle-and-thread—which grow in mixed stands with

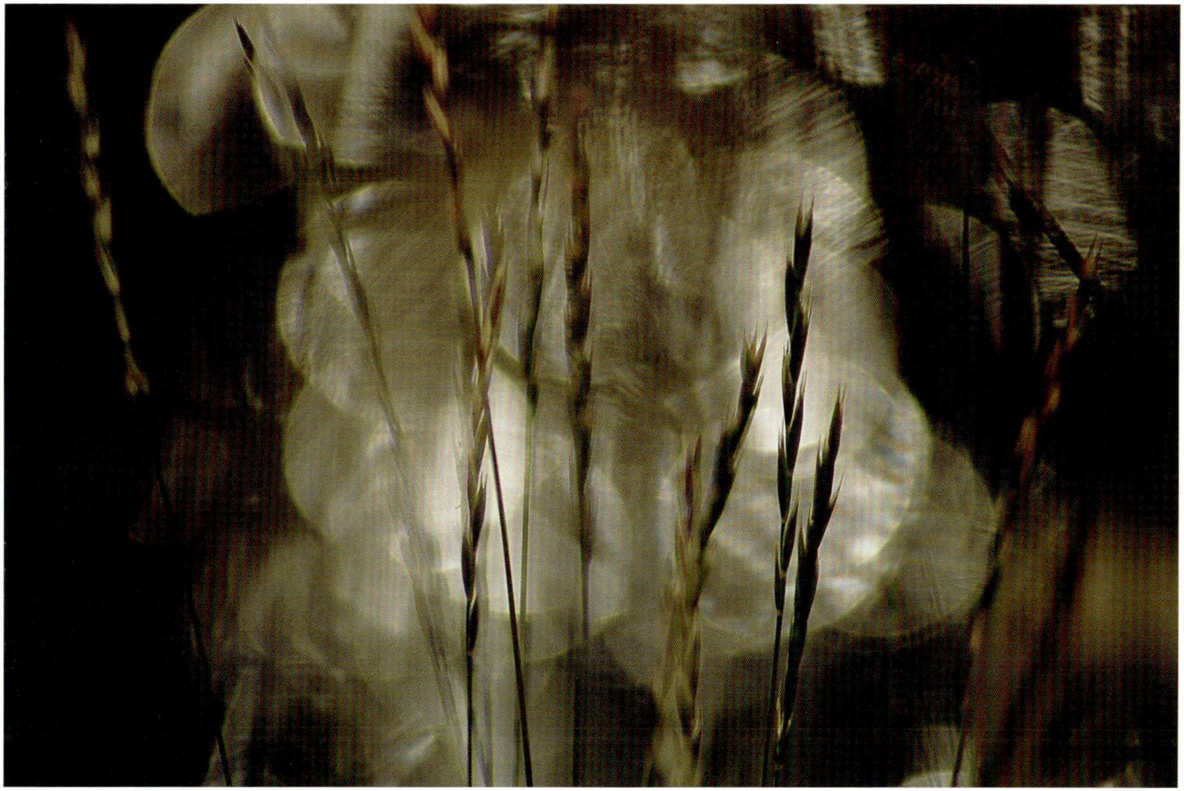

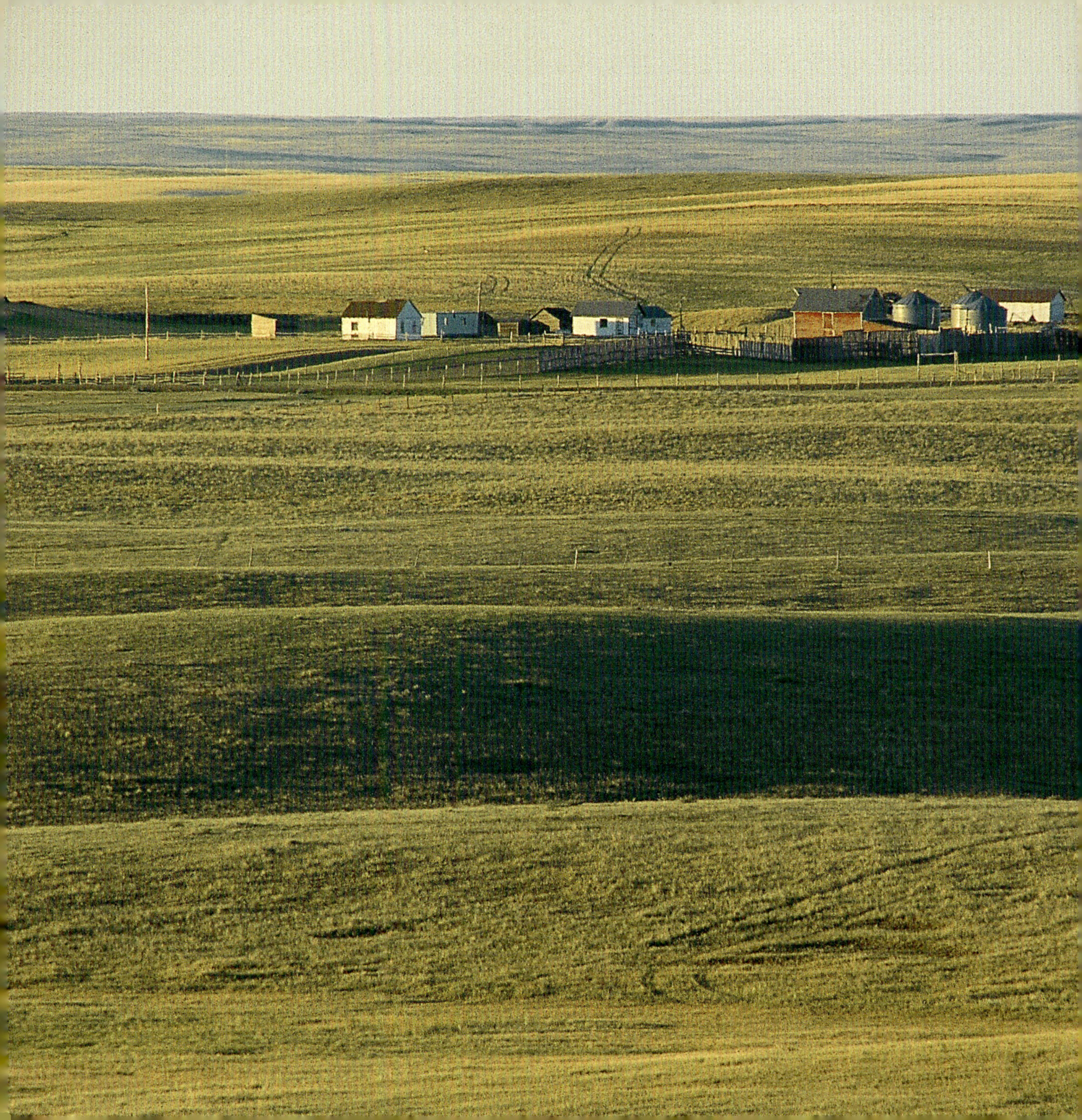

Left: The Butala homestead, representing two generations of hard labour, is merely a dot in this huge landscape.

Either for feeding their livestock or for recreation, a few ranchers have gone back to using teams of heavy horses as their grandfathers did.

short grasses, chiefly blue grama (*Bouteloua gracilis*) with its delicate, eyebrow-shaped head. A field of grass in excellent condition is to a rancher's eye more beautiful than a bed of blooming hothouse roses. Maintaining that beauty requires skill and technical knowledge and, in such dry country with its not very fruitful soils, a willingness to put the quality of the grass ahead of the need to make a profit.

There are no laws in place to prevent a landowner from overgrazing, or from ploughing his remaining native prairie in order either to plant a foreign grass species or to seed it to cereal or oilseed crops. Saskatchewan government policy with regard to leased lands, the ownership of which remains with the province, changes in response to prevailing ideas about land

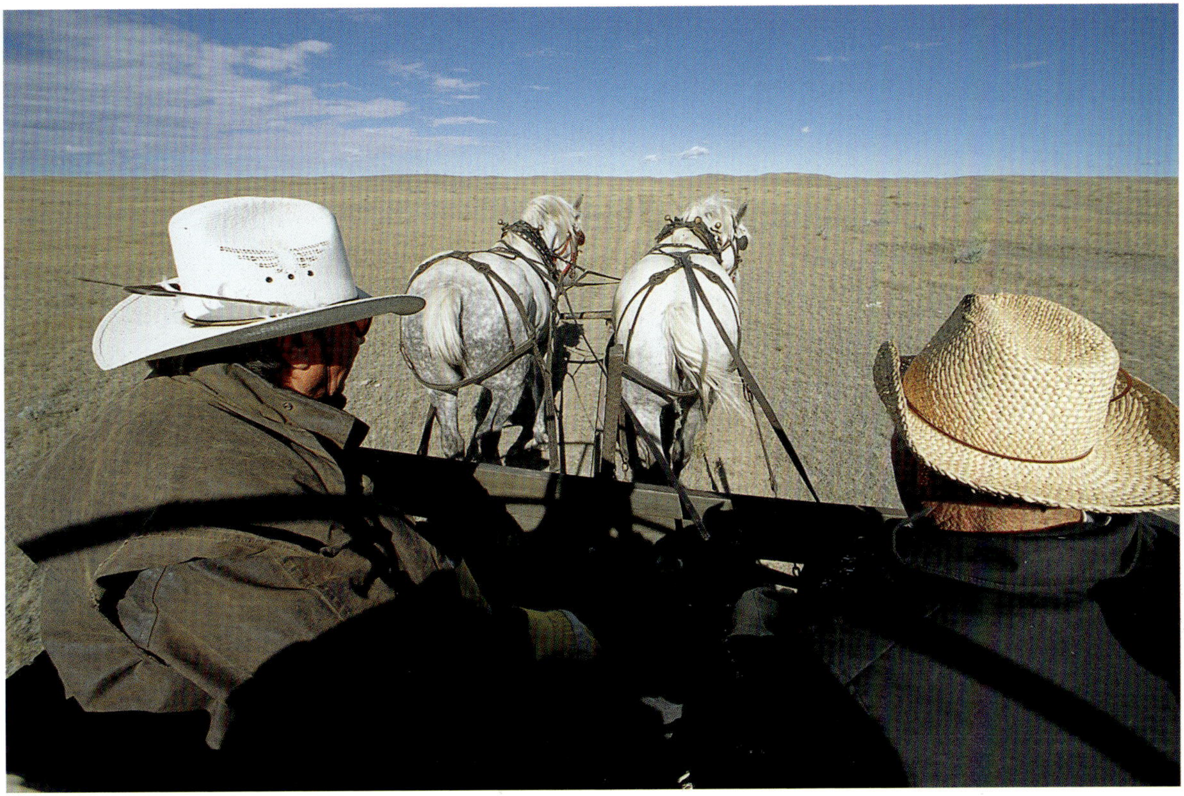

management, but currently the policy is that no land leased from the province may be ploughed.

Certainly there are ranchers today who succeed in keeping their grass uninvaded and in good condition, but there are also those who overstock in order to raise the family income, or in order to pay ever-increasing land taxes and grazing fees. Sometimes, as with the occasional acreage owner, overgrazing is caused simply by a lack of knowledge as to how best to manage grazing land. A "windshield survey" on country roads in Western Canada or the western United States will reveal in short order just how widespread, and often severe, this problem is.

All this Peter taught me as I rode for days with him, chasing cows home in the fall and out in the spring, or herding them, lying on hillsides watching them go for water or graze. Slowly, ever so slowly, and to this day twenty-five years later, the process is still not complete, Peter taught me to live in the rhythm of nature. Rather than by clock or calendar, my days are measured

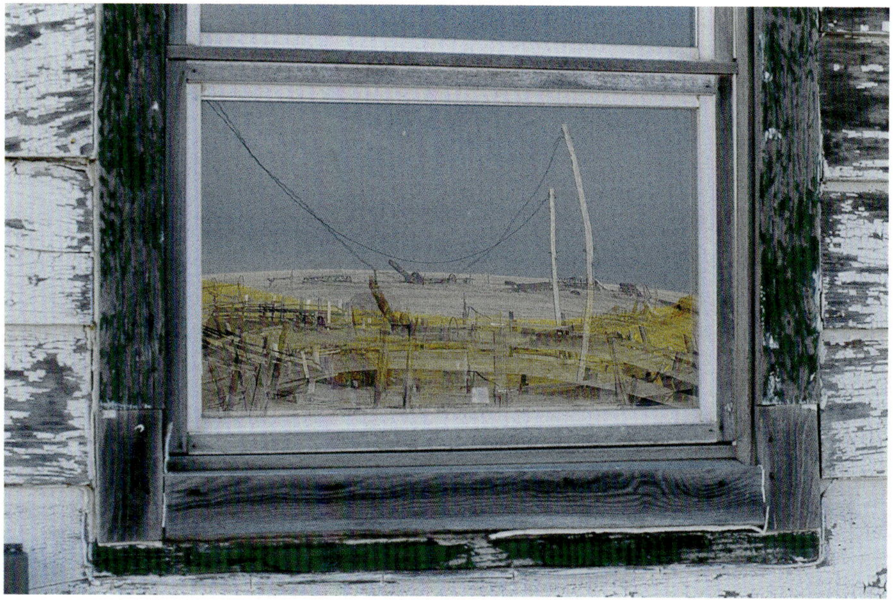

This surreal view of images superimposed on images is produced by the warp in this homestead window glass.

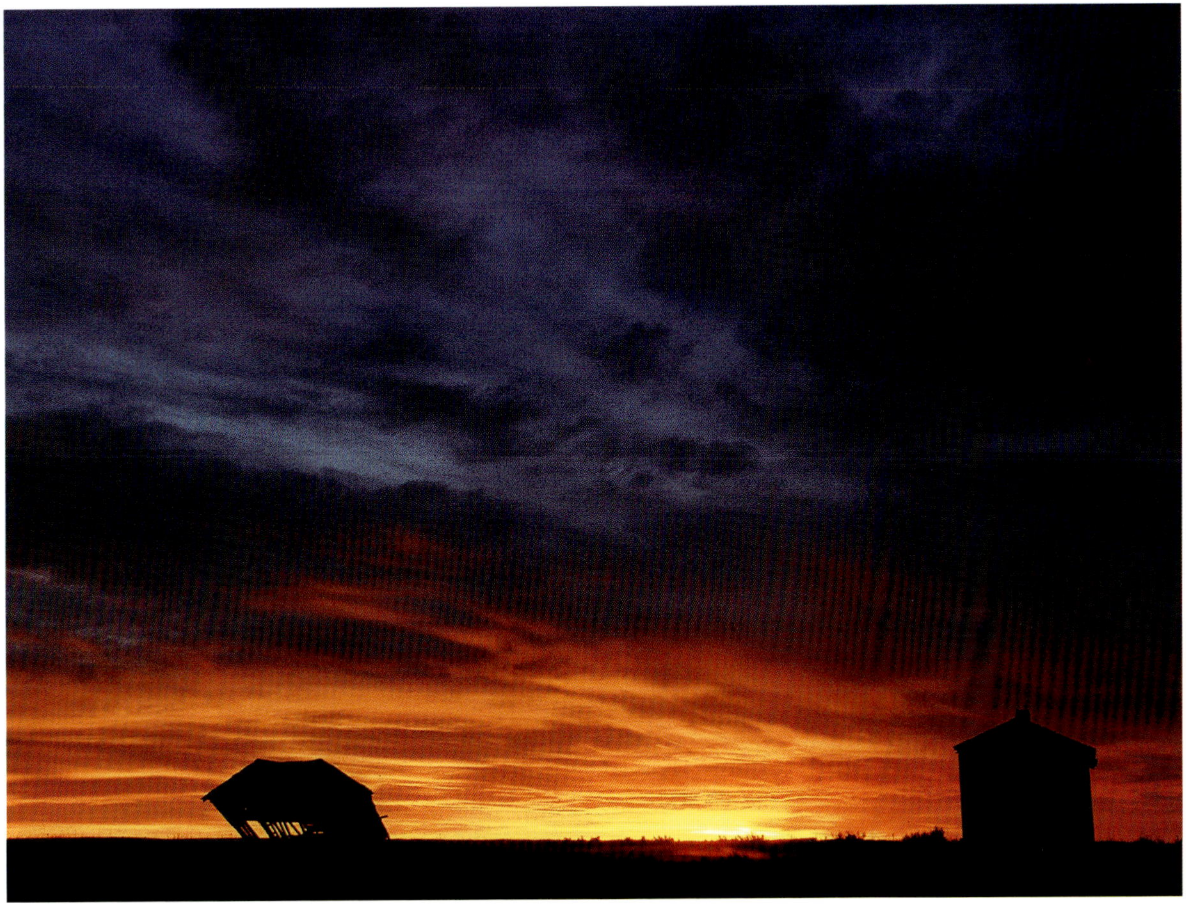

Sunsets in Western Canada are spectacular.

by the rising and setting of the sun, and my nights by the passage of the moon, the years by the slow turning of the seasons. He taught me the necessity of working with the weather, to the extent that anyone with cattle and horses to look after can. I began to be afraid of lightning, to head for home at its first sign, because now I'd seen the corpses of cattle and horses killed by it as they grazed their inoffensive way across the prairie. I began to see the livability of the average winter storm—not the harsh ones—because Peter and I went out in them, especially in the spring, to make sure the cows and their calves were moving to shelter, and to chase off the odd coyote waiting patiently for its chance to pick off an unguarded calf. I began to appreciate the way the prairie came to life after rain, as myriad small flowers sprang into bloom right after a rainstorm.

In practical, daily ways, as well as through my abundant nightly dreaming, I was learning how nature works, not so much in obvious ways, as to what I might expect of a killing winter storm or a summer drought or heat wave, but in more subtle ways. I began to see something larger: that behind these daily or seasonal vicissitudes nature was entirely serene. I began to see it as omnipresent, as all-powerful, and we humans, with our sense of control, as puny, arrogant, and in the face of it, and despite our delusions of might, essentially helpless.

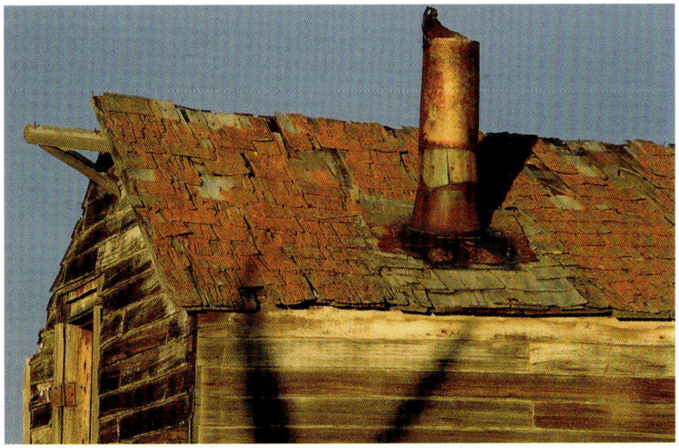

The Settlers

In 1872, the Canadian government enacted the Dominion Lands Act which enabled settlers, for $10, to take up 160 acres or a quarter section (the section of 640 acres—one mile by one mile—being the basic land measurement) in Canada's North-West Territories, today the provinces Alberta, Saskatchewan, and Manitoba. Fifty-six million acres in Western Canada were eventually taken up as free homesteads, and later, through a variety of programs, a further 60 million acres were made available for purchase. The days of free passage over the open prairies were gone forever.

I came from families which, on all sides, were among the settlers. Until I moved to the ranch to live and began my walking on the prairie, I had no other version of history, at least none that I could take seriously, than that of our pioneering past. I saw the settlers as noble, as heroic, as I'd been taught, and the work that they had done to tame the wild prairie as just and right. It didn't occur to me to question this. Our fathers and grandfathers essentially wanted to make a living off the land; our mothers and grandmothers wanted to domesticate it—they wanted flowers and vegetables from it, and grass to

A decrepit settler's shack turns splendid in the prairie's golden light.

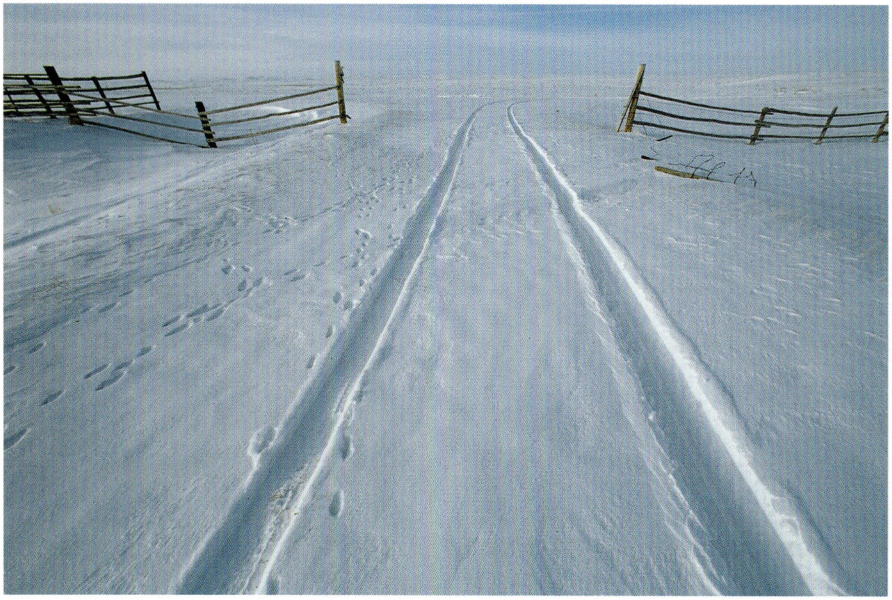

Only rabbit and tire tracks mark the winter landscape.

fatten a milch cow. Nobody I know of wanted wilderness, wanted nature just as they found it.

It was not until at the age of thirty-six, when I married Peter and moved to his ranch to live, that I began to learn a different way of seeing land. True, it was still essentially a history-less land: that is, a land whose history had begun around the year 1900. But it was from Peter's attitude that I began to question the one I had learned from my mother and grandmother—the "necessary" transformation of the prairie—and my understanding of this new approach to land was intensified and deepened by my solitary, questioning walks across it.

The promise of owning their own land brought hundreds of thousands of people to Western Canada from as far away as remote villages in Eastern Europe. In the Divide-Claydon area (the once-thriving little towns that flank the OMB), this stage began around 1910, somewhat later than the rest of the province, reportedly because settlers preferred to live close to the

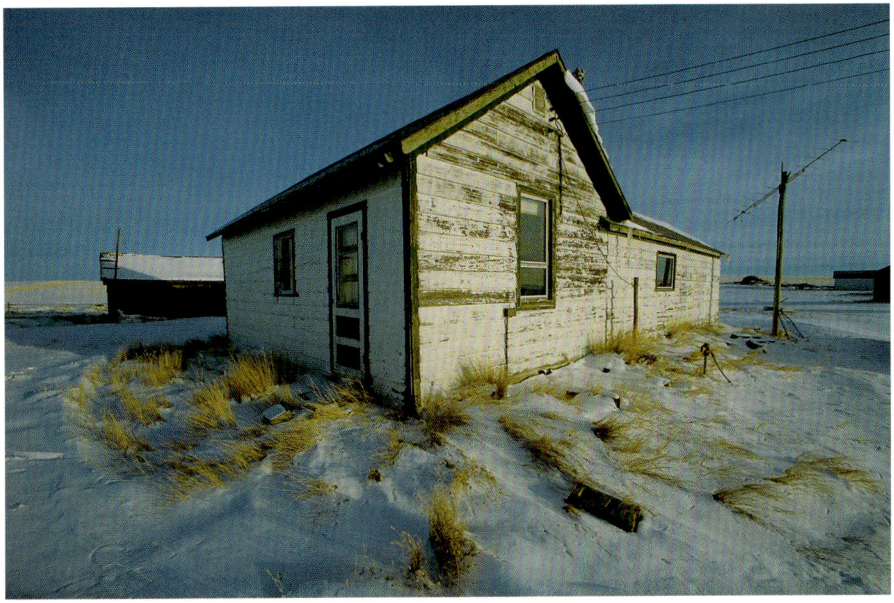

The human struggle for survival, the constant effort to stay ahead of the elements, takes place in the midst of an eternal prairie.

main railway line. As more and more of the best and the closest land was claimed, settlers had to go farther and farther afield, and onto less desirable claims.

As they began to arrive in large numbers, they put increasing pressure on the federal government to make available as much land as possible for farming—all of which the settlers claimed, sometimes foolishly, to be arable. This included the vast grazing leases of the ranchers. In 1892, the government capitulated and made provision for settlers to homestead on ranchers' grazing lands, and in response to the ranchers' obvious concerns, allowed them to purchase up to one-tenth of their leases at $1.25 per acre (later $2). Although some of the big ranches survived the loss of their grazing leases by buying the 10 per cent allowed them, and then buying more land from the railroads, in Saskatchewan, as the settlers flooded in, most big ranches collapsed to an unremarkable size. Just as the hegemony of the Aboriginal people with their ethic of communal land finally ended, so did the days of

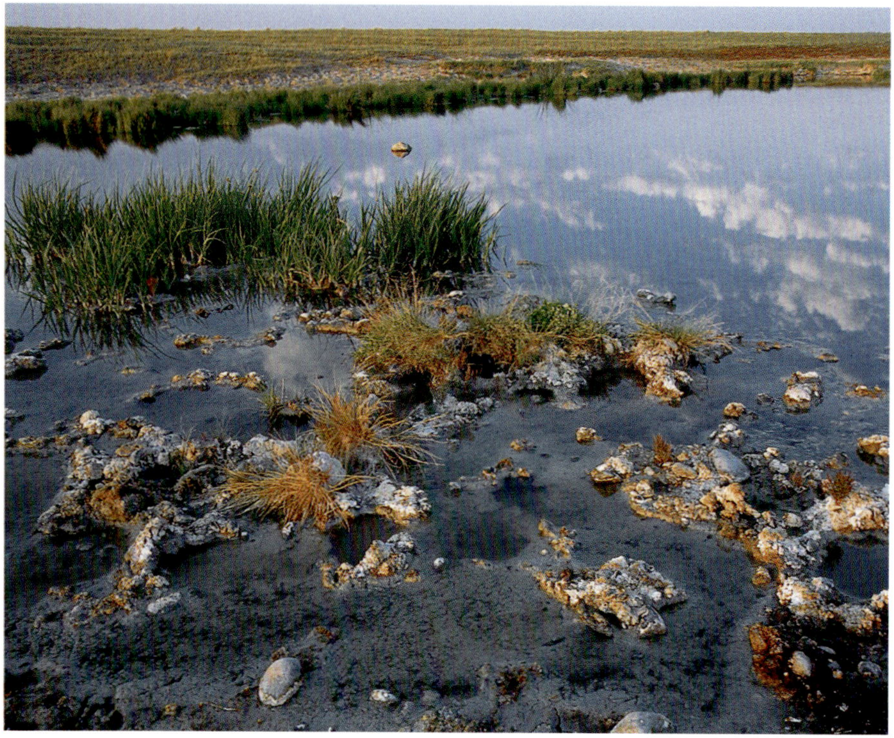

This spring-fed wetland is the only permanent and natural source of water on the OMB.

the kingdom of grass, and of ranching with its unique land ethic as the prevailing way of life on the grasslands. The era of farming, with its new ethic of land as private property, had begun.

If today the traveller were to stop on the northeast quarter of section 18, he would see a field of native grass sloping down to the north and east with a vast view of countryside all the way to Claydon eight miles east, and on clear days, well beyond to the towns of Loomis and Frontier. A search in the grass would show a depression with a few large stones lying in disarray around its perimeter where a house once stood, and his quick eye would discern in the trampled grass a fragment of faded, discoloured glass, a flattened and rusted pot or a tin can, or a bolt or an unidentifiable piece of iron from an outdated farming implement, all clues to the fact that this was once a homestead.

A few yards to the north, two more depressions in a low hillside would reveal to the traveller that there was once a dugout barn here and possibly a second outbuilding. To the south and west of these depressions, he would see grassed ridges of earth, small man-made dams, now broken, which would have provided water for livestock and a vegetable garden. To the east, he would see a few inches-high, non-native shrubs—caraganas—that must once have formed a protective hedge, where today the sun and the wind sweep freely over the open countryside. And farther east a really acute eye can pick out in a field of native grass the land that at least eighty-five years ago a homesteader ploughed (demonstrating that once cultivated, then simply abandoned, the prairie doesn't return to exactly what it was before). There is nothing left of years of hard labour but these few scattered remains.

Except for one more remnant: on the highest point of the quarter there is an oval-shaped iris bed, with an adjoining small circle at one end, in all perhaps eight feet long. The plants are impacted and tiny, but very much alive. No one can explain this, no one remembers the irises being planted there, no one knows by whom, nor why, since it is in the least sheltered location, and far from the buildings, making it a long way to carry water. That these tiny plants are still alive, no one having tended to them or watered them in nearly seventy years, is the greatest mystery of all.

This was once the place of Hannah and Henry Nursall, a couple who came to Saskatchewan from England around 1915, when they were already in their fifties. Mr. Nursall had been in the British army in India; she is remembered as a midwife who delivered at least two of the settlers' children. It was 1928 before the Nursalls received title to their homestead quarter, a testament to the difficulty of making a living in such arid country. But they stayed twenty years, and only in 1935 did they leave for Regina, where Henry died the following year. In 1937, Mrs. Nursall, who had by this time moved to White Rock, B.C., died also, and was buried there.

Their granddaughter, Irene Hopkins, spent fifteen or more summers as a child on what became the OMB. She recalls that in the twenties and early thirties there were neighbours on most quarter sections. They had come from places as varied as Iowa and the Dakotas in the United States, the Pyrenees of France and Spain, the British Isles, Scandinavia, and Slovakia, and lived side by side, under the same conditions, in this new country. During the epic drought of the thirties, life was so difficult that the government opened settlements farther north and helped settlers to move there. All told, on the roughly twenty square miles of the OMB (more than eighty quarters) there have been only twelve settlers, out of a mere dozen and a half, who managed to obtain title to their homestead quarters, and none stayed on those homesteads as long as the Nursalls did.

Today, the more than 13,000 acres of the OMB—windswept, echoing now only with the call of birds and the occasional cry of coyotes—are uninhabited. The era of settlers sweeping into the country with dreams of conquest and glory had by the forties, for many in the OMB area, ended in heartbreak. Its peak had lasted only about thirty years. When you consider that it has been only about ninety years since the arrival of the first settlers, compared to the 14,000 years since the last Ice Age's melt-back, it is barely the blink of an eye.

And yet, as with the Nursall place, the traces of the settlers' occupation remain to this day in the form of changes to the surface of the land: depressions in the ground, low ridges where early farming implements did their work, embankments that were dams, or ditches for drainage, the detritus of homestead life still scattered on the prairie, stunted hedges of introduced shrubs and trees in a naturally treeless land, and the changing of the plant life on the place where they onced lived and farmed.

Today, all the land of the west is marked in squares, and identified and owned by someone, and no stranger has the right to walk or ride anywhere, other than on roads or in areas set aside as parks, without someone's permission. Peter's father, George Butala, was fond of telling the story of how he once rode on horseback all the way from the Old Man On His Back to the Sweetgrass Hills in Montana "without opening a gate." By this he meant that

As these artifacts of the settler era slowly disintegrate, they take on a surprising beauty.

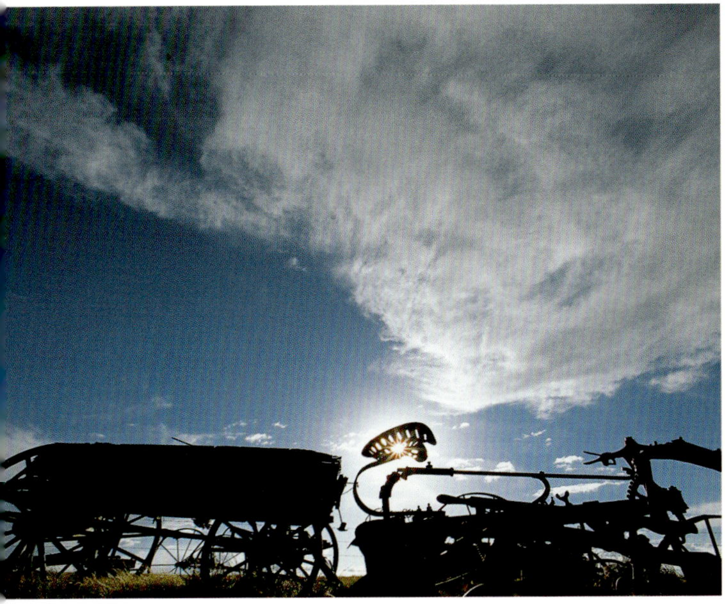

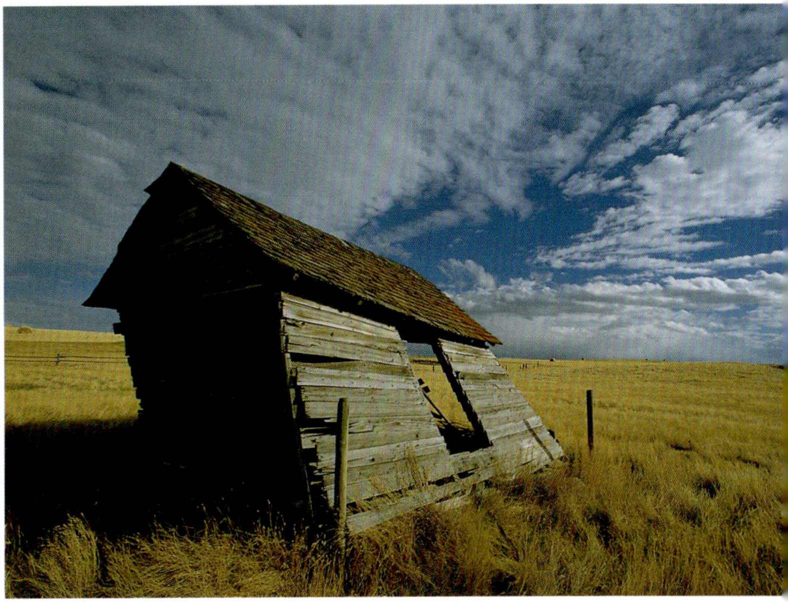

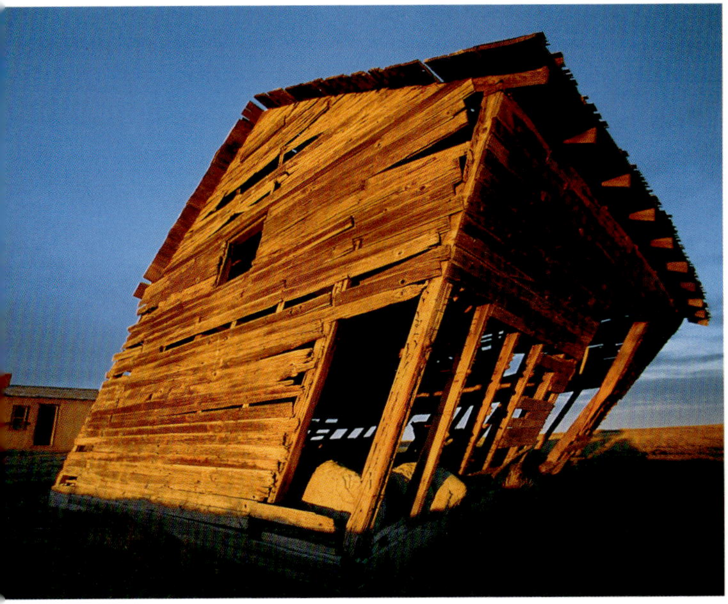

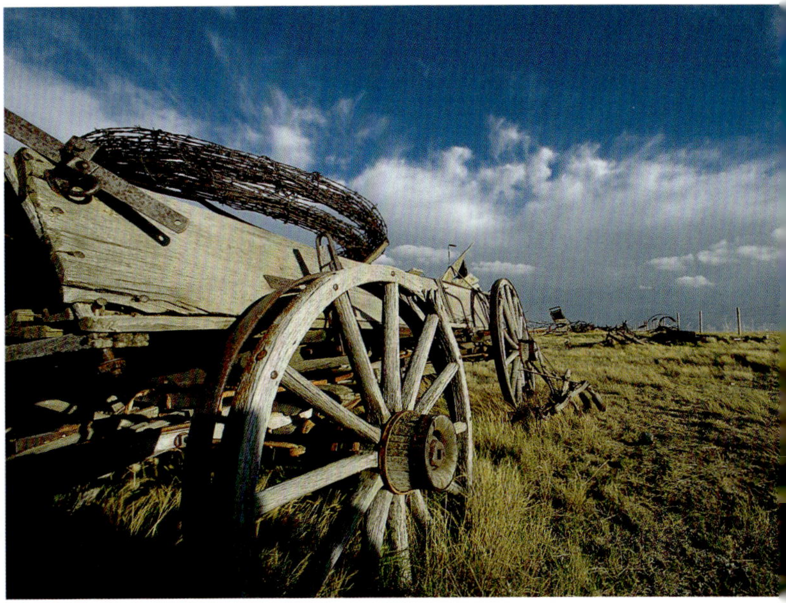

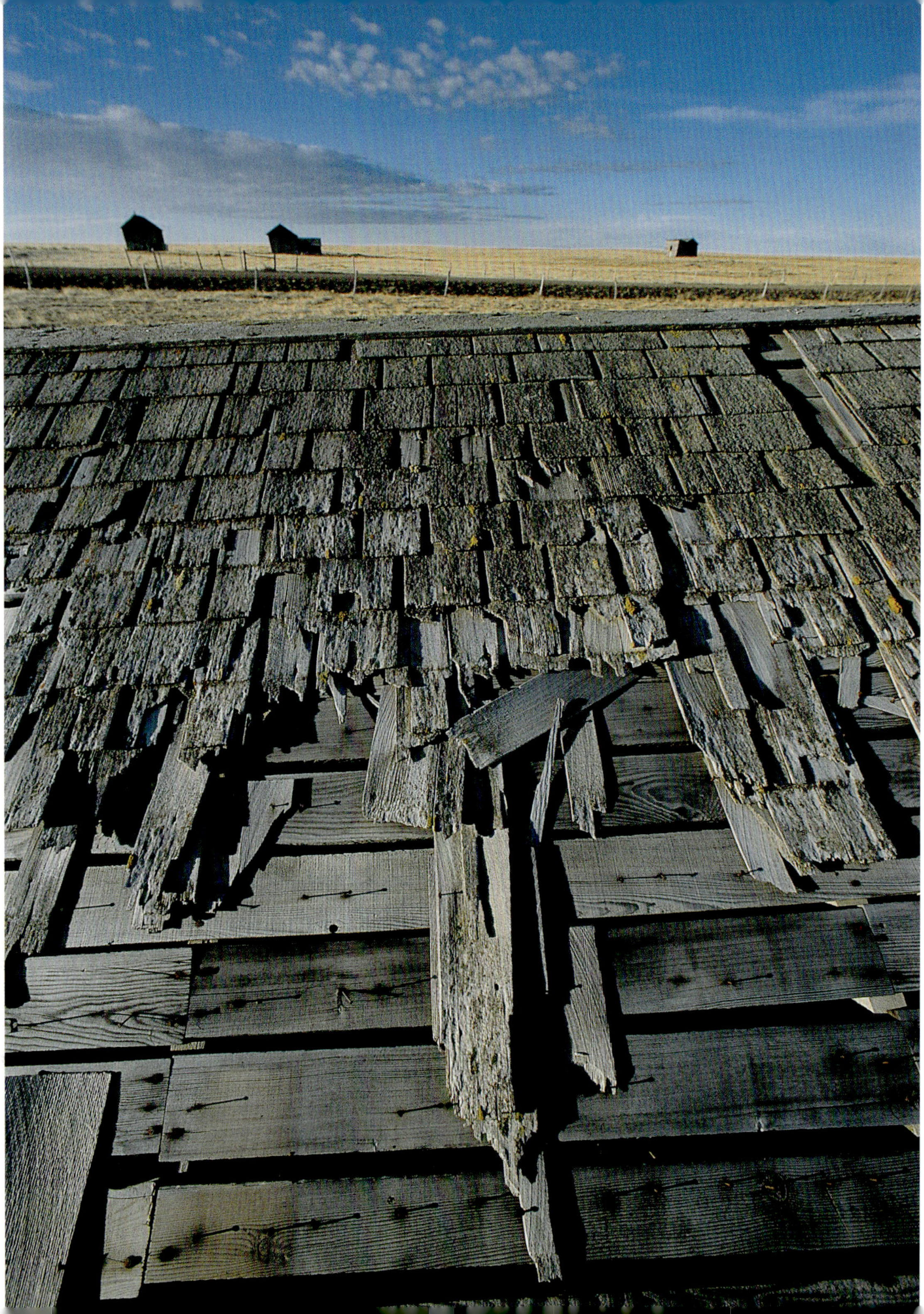

the land was unfenced all that way, and that anyone might ride across it. With the arrival of the settlers, and to the grief of the Aboriginal people and the old-style cowboys, the days of the open prairie had ended.

The early style of farming remained, sometimes by default—given small equipment, the small farms, the ability of the farmer to be intimately acquainted with his few acres—somewhat environmentally friendly. But the farmers of an earlier time farmed not only to make a living, and to feel free as they never could as salaried workers, but often also because they were in love with life lived on the land, in the countryside, in the presence of nature in all its manifestations. It was undeniably a hard life, requiring the labour of everyone from the youngest child to the aged grandparents, and it was lived usually in poverty, with endlessly long days, backbreaking labour, and much hardship, from failed crops to desperate loneliness. It is no wonder that we hold the pioneers in reverence. Still, we should not forget that they were occupiers, whether they recognized it or not, of Aboriginal lands, and that their very presence, innocent of malicious intent and instigated by the government as it was, had caused much greater hardship and suffering to an entire people.

As I walked the grassland day after day, year after year, people around us were continuing to plough the prairie in order to seed crops. It looked, some days, as if in no time there'd be no prairie left at all. It was surprising to me to find that even today the largest area of intact—at least, unploughed—native prairie remains in southwestern Saskatchewan. In 1996, approximately half the land (some estimates are as low as 30 per cent) in the southwestern corner of the province was in its natural state (not all of which would be grassland). The Saskatchewan Wetland Conservation Corporation estimates that there are about 15 million acres of native prairie left in Saskatchewan out of an original 67 million acres, but it also points out that in areas where the land is well suited to crop production—the dark brown and black soil zones in particular—less than 2 per cent remains in native prairie.

Settlers didn't arrive on the OMB until about 1912 due to its distance from the railway.

Unfortunately, something like 84 per cent of the remaining native prairie (in these better zones) consists of properties under 160 acres in size, hardly viable either for wildlife or for prairie plant communities which are thought to require a minimum of 200 acres to maintain their ecological balance. But, worst of all, 40 per cent of them are smaller than 40 acres, a size not viable for prairie plant communities, or for most wildlife either. And even these small parcels of grass are threatened by a number of pressures: their potential as cropland or as acreages, too-heavy grazing, the advance of exotic plant species, and the presence of gravel for roads.

The government's intention in bringing settlers to Western Canada was that the newcomers would grow crops for market, not merely in order to

An abandoned piano speaks of a vanished way of life.

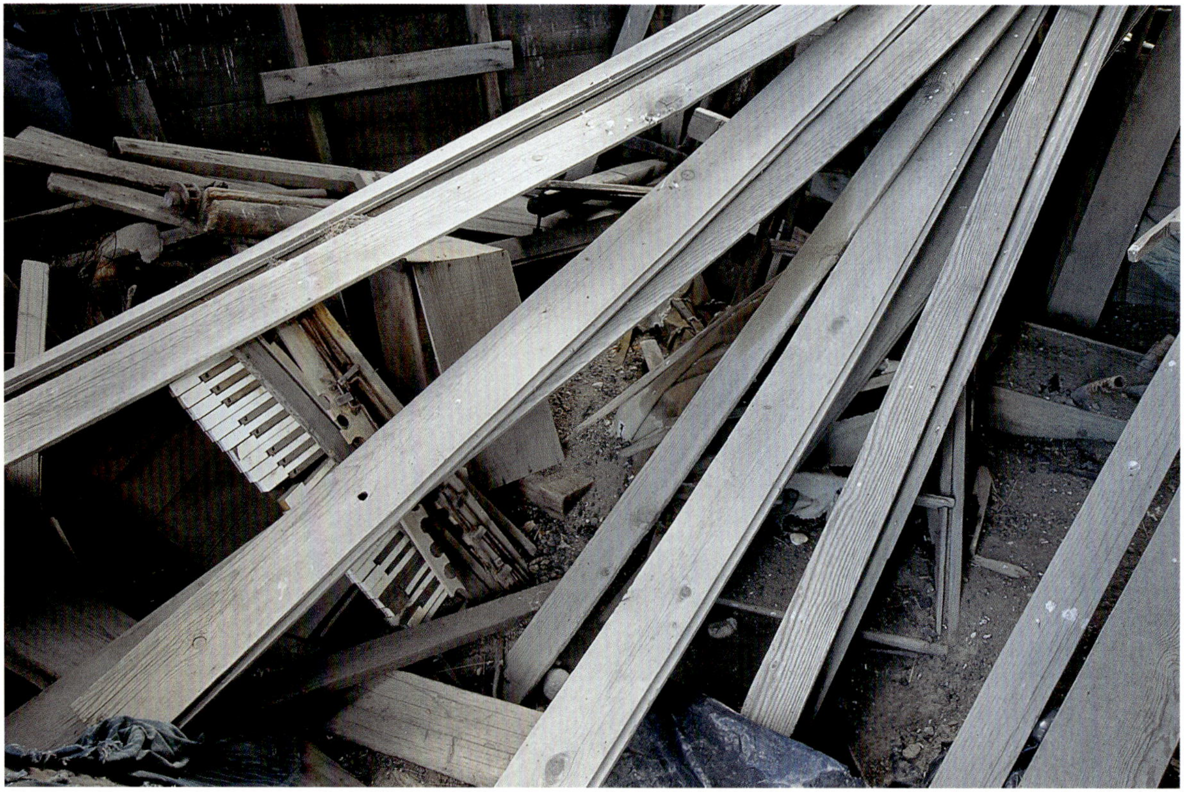

sustain themselves and their families, as many of them had done in the countries from which they came. This imperative—that the sale of a farmer's crop would provide the bulk of his living—set the scene for today's large-scale modern farms that have so drastically altered the grasslands.

This new style, brought about by advances in farming technology, and in part by globalization of the world economy, results in huge farms. Large farms, of course, require substantial mechanization, which in turn requires huge amounts of money, usually in the form of loans. If few others do, financial institutions certainly flourish in such a system.

Holdings of thousands of acres require large-scale solutions to problems such as weeds and the presence of obstacles—sloughs, small hills and coulees, trees—in the path of equipment. Since the Second World War, such solutions have included the repeated applications of noxious chemical sprays, which unfortunately also indiscriminately kill wildlife. The problem of "obstacles" in the way of machines is solved by the bulldozer, an instrument of no great delicacy. Such a farming style requires a lot of crossed fingers that science will be able to keep ahead of the problems it causes: the loss of fertility of overfarmed soil, the loss of soil fibre, and the compaction of the soil by heavy equipment. In fact, this agricultural style is expressive of the newer view of land as itself a commodity, as a private resource to be used—despite good intentions in the form of the application of chemical fertilizers, zero-till agriculture, and other modifications—presumably, until it is used up.

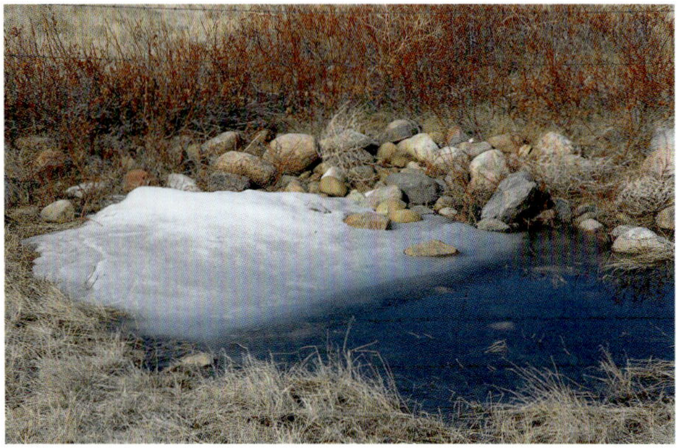

The Uses of Land

If both the farmer and the rancher tend to see the value of native prairie primarily in terms of its use to them as a way to make a living, the developer, of course, is unabashed in this approach. If a piece of land is beautiful enough, even its remoteness can be seen as an asset in monetary terms. It can be promoted and sold as a wilderness hideaway to the thousands of affluent urban people who yearn to return to nature. The OMB isn't in immediate danger of this happening, largely because there is no lake or river nearby, no airport, no trees for shade or firewood, no water supply of sufficient quantity for a large development, nor of high enough quality for most acreage owners. On the other hand, none of these obstacles is insurmountable. As beautiful places far from crowds of people or industrial development become harder and harder to find, it is not beyond the possible to imagine such an eventual fate—that of mere real estate—for any unprotected grasslands of southwestern Saskatchewan.

The scientist, however, takes another view. He sees a stunning and, for Canadian grassland, rare display of flourishing biodiversity, on which opportunities abound for learning more about how such mixed-grass prairie

In spring, an adequate winter snowfall will bring a welcome supply of clean, fresh water.

works in an ecological sense, as well as how smaller plant communities, and individual plants, go about executing their genetic programming. As well, the very biodiversity present, which includes a number of rare plants, provides a scientist with the opportunity to study the possibilities inherent in various plants for food and medicines. And the ecology of such a piece of land includes the insects that inhabit it, the larger animals, and the birds.

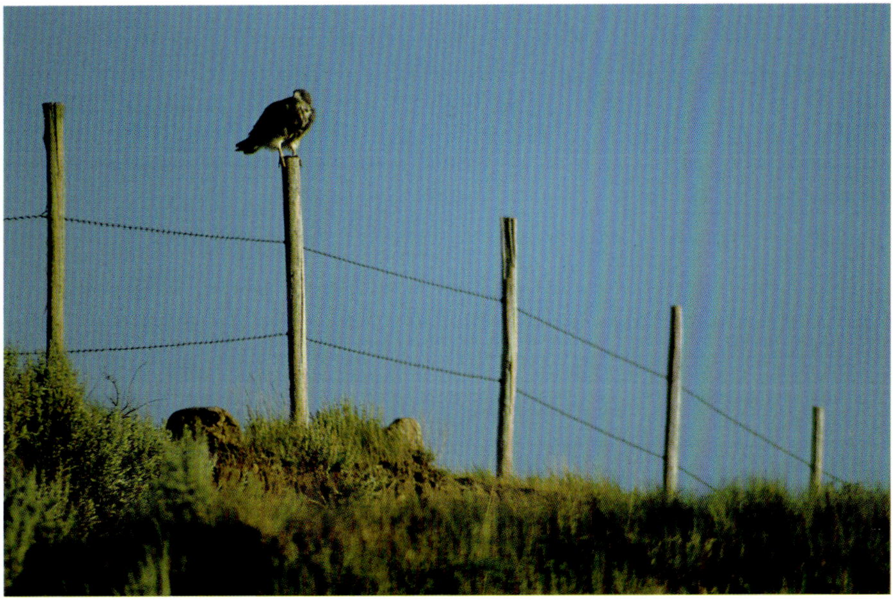

The ferruginous hawk, another native species that is at risk, is encouraged to breed on the OMB.

If the arrival of Europeans destroyed the ancient way of life of the Aboriginal people of the Great Plains, it also had drastic effects on the area's wildlife. Beginning with the Hudson's Bay Company's insatiable need for beaver pelts for fashionable Europeans, then extending to other animals, and ending with today's mega-farms which leave virtually no wildlife habitat at all, native animals have had a hard time of it. The Plains grizzly was lost in the nineteenth century, driven into the mountains, it is thought, and the last Plains wolf was seen around 1935, allowing the coyote to expand in numbers to fill its niche. The black-footed ferret has been extirpated from

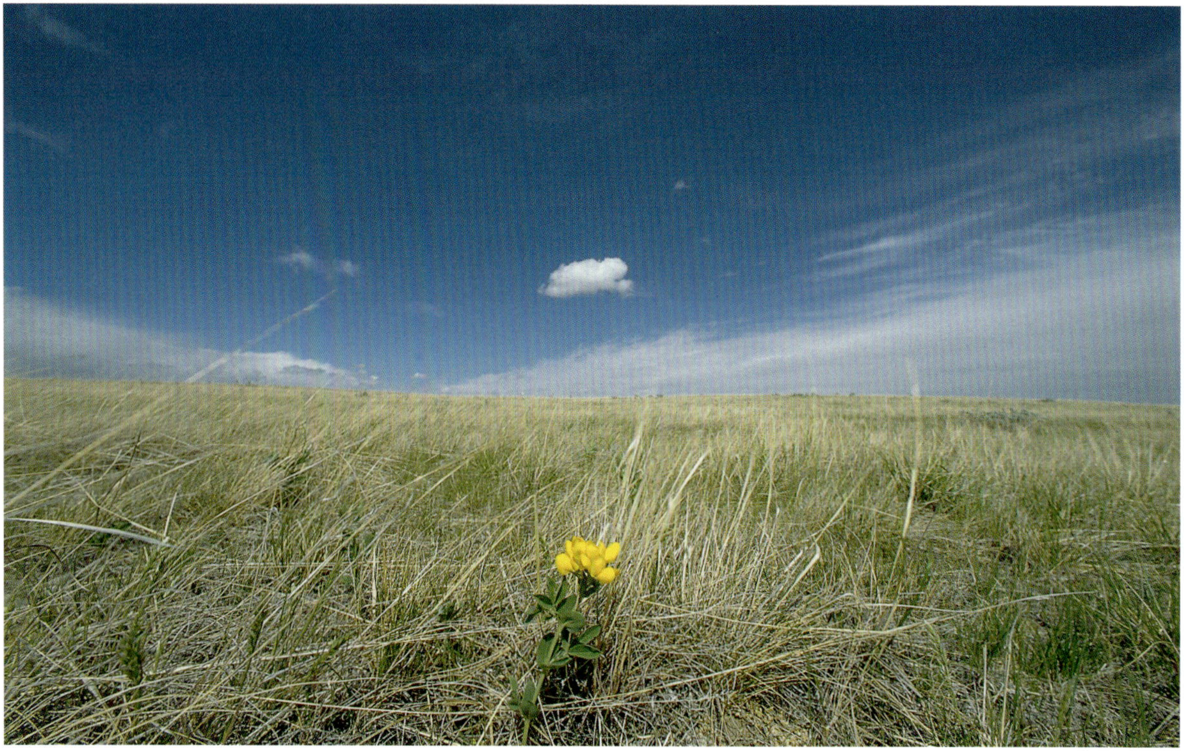

this area, as well as the once ubiquitous swift fox, currently being reintroduced (but seen by the settlers as something of a curse), and the ferruginous hawk and burrowing owl are endangered, the latter severely so.

Non-conservation-minded people have trouble understanding why some will fight to preserve one rare species of plant or animal, thinking them deluded and self-dramatizing. Yet, if one species is allowed to go, the next week another is allowed to disappear, and then another, and another. Each time, a genetic heritage that can never be repeated or replaced vanishes from the earth. And even if as humans we had no known use for that particular species, the time might come when we would. But before even thinking of "use," there is the question of rights: *What right have humans to obliterate a part of creation?*

Some ranchers say you shouldn't put your cattle out to graze before the buffalo bean, or golden bean, blooms.

Right: In part because of decreasing habitat, pronghorn numbers—except on the OMB—have declined.

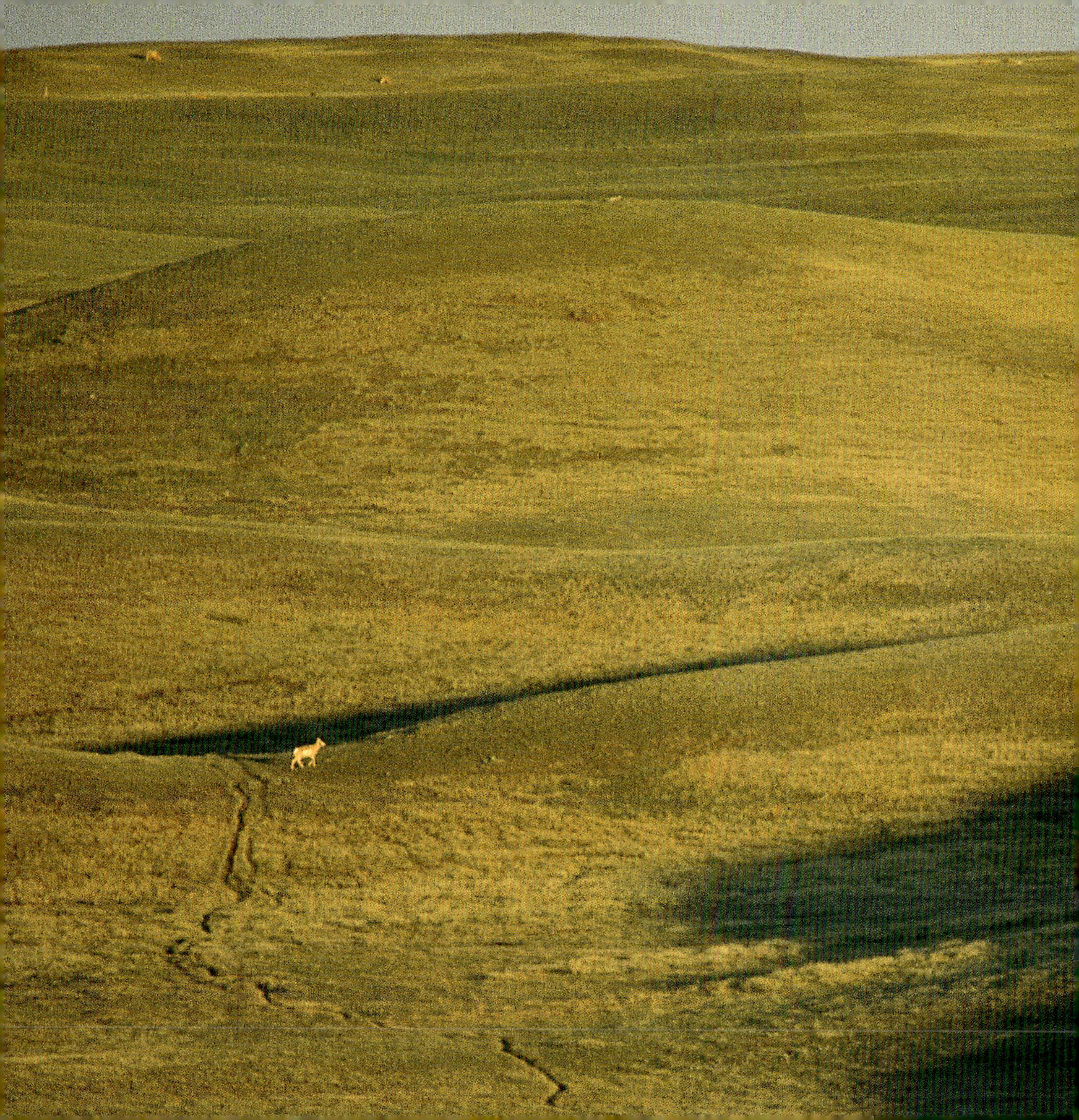

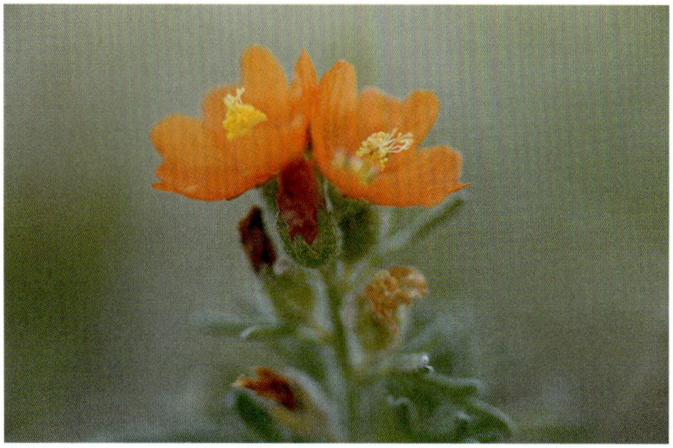

Old Man On His Back

The topography and soils of the OMB were formed by the glaciers as they melted and left behind deposits of till (rocks, gravel, dirt), forming three landscapes: in the north, hummocky moraine—high hills, up to 998 metres, with sloughs between them caused by deposits from the glacier as it melted—probably not arable even today; in the central part, till plain—a more gently undulating surface, the result of the glacier leaving fewer deposits than in the north—probably arable; in the south, dissected plateau—valley complexes with large, uneroded blocks of plateau—much of it arable—and the valley bottoms (as low as 915 metres) carved out by glacial meltwater. Although much of the OMB was once too hilly to be ploughed, today, with modern four-wheel-drive tractors and other new inventions, most of the OMB could be worked as farmland.

But the kind and depth of topsoil is also a determining factor in what is farmed and what isn't—information not available to those first settlers who, if they hadn't been farmers previously, might not have understood if they had had it. On the OMB, the soil types are poorer quality Brown Chernozemic, saline soils called Solonetzic, and soils called Gleysolic, that is,

If there is enough moisture in spring, patches of prairie will be gaily carpeted with the orange-red scarlet mallow, which can last into July.

Right: Views of unfenced grassland are becoming increasingly rare.

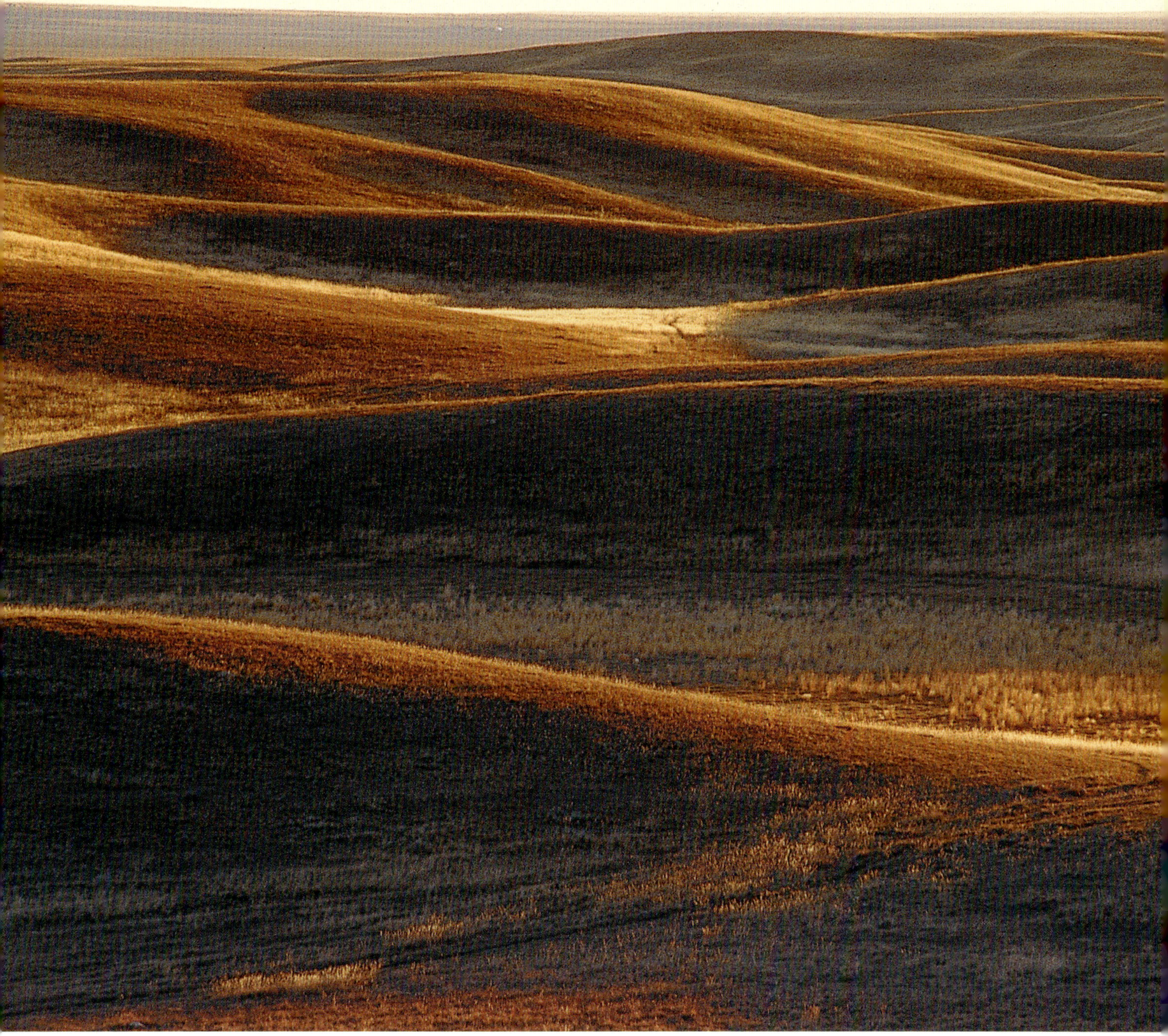

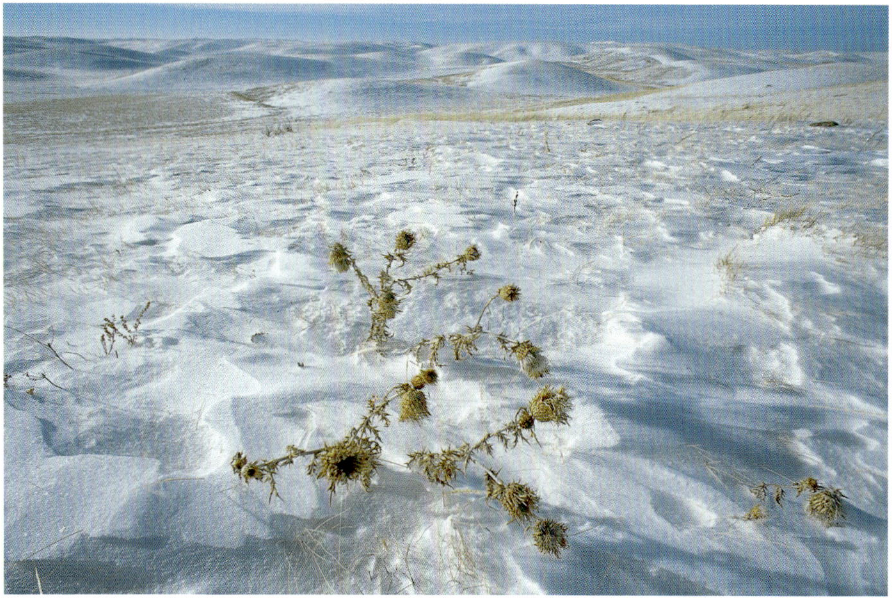

Winter on the OMB has its own beauty.

waterlogged with poor drainage. All of these were formed in glacial till, incorporating some Cretaceous shales and also some Tertiary bedrock substances. These are mostly class-five soils, out of a possible six, with class one being the best farming soil. Class five is described by scientists as having severe limitations in terms of cereal grains cropping. Such soils are also limited by inadequate precipitation during the growing season, and are described as best suited to carefully managed grazing.

As for the depth of topsoil, the layer of glacial till in the southwest is thinner than elsewhere in the province. Often the bedrock is bare, occasionally even down to the previous period, the Cretaceous, in which the bones of dinosaurs are found. Thus, for the most part, there is little surface soil, especially compared to that of the province's better farming areas, where it might be as much as several feet deep.

Despite the fact that land much like it is farmed year after year, it is clear that this isn't its best use. Yet the only law governing how a farmer uses the land he owns is the Noxious Weeds Act, which requires him to control certain plants seen in agriculture as weeds. If he owns the land, he may plough the least fertile of soils, or land containing the best habitat for any species of plant or animal. The farmer believes that the need to grow food outweighs virtually any other consideration, and given the burgeoning population of the world, there has always been much reason to endorse this attitude, as well as to applaud the enormous success of North American farmers in meeting this demand. It is only now, in the early twenty-first century, that serious concerns arise about the concomitant and expanding destruction of the diversity of life forms, both plant and animal, as a result of an ethic driven chiefly by the international marketplace.

Following pages: Gorgeous as this sky is, most ranchers prefer to view it through a window, because lightning kills.

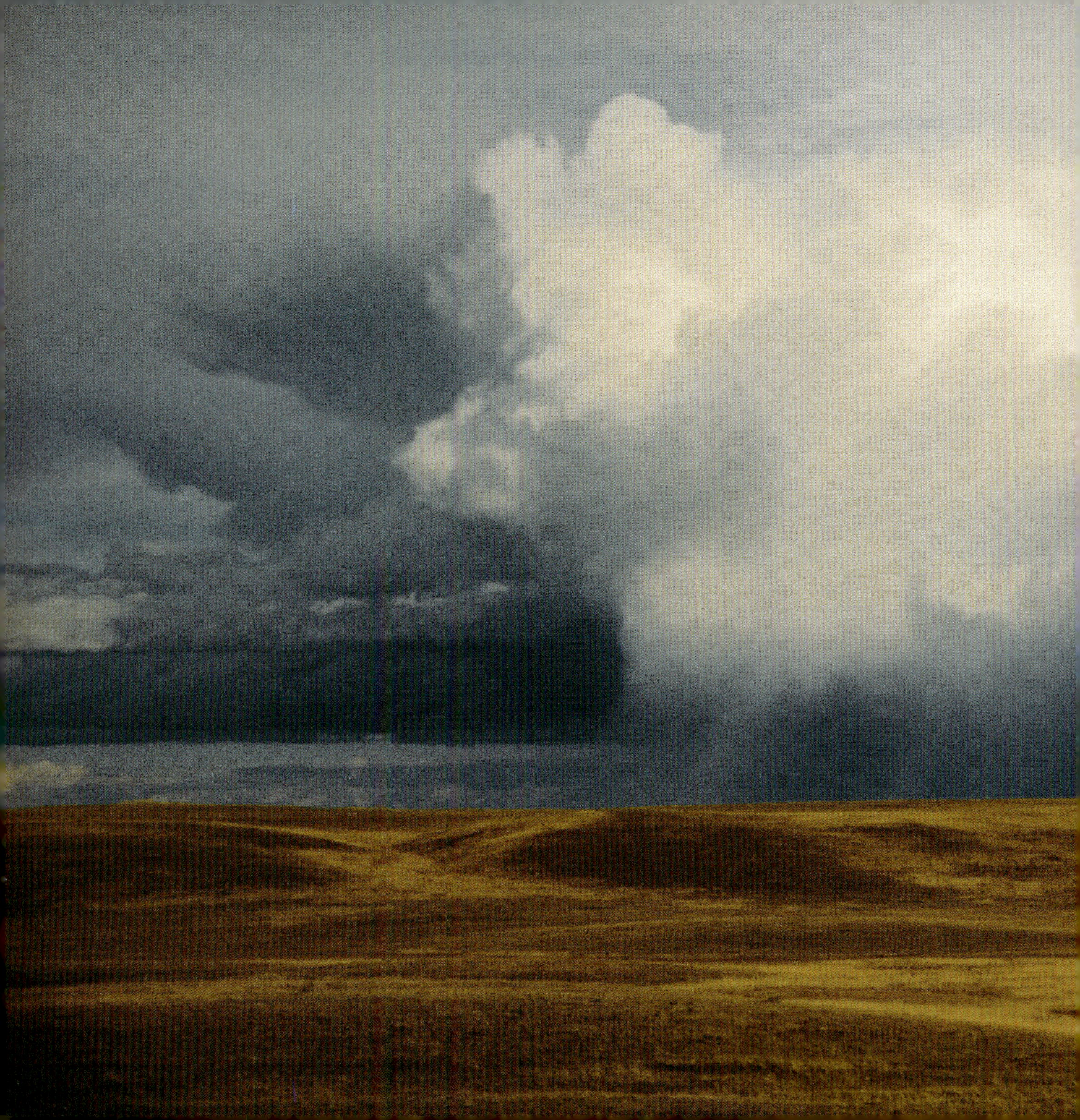

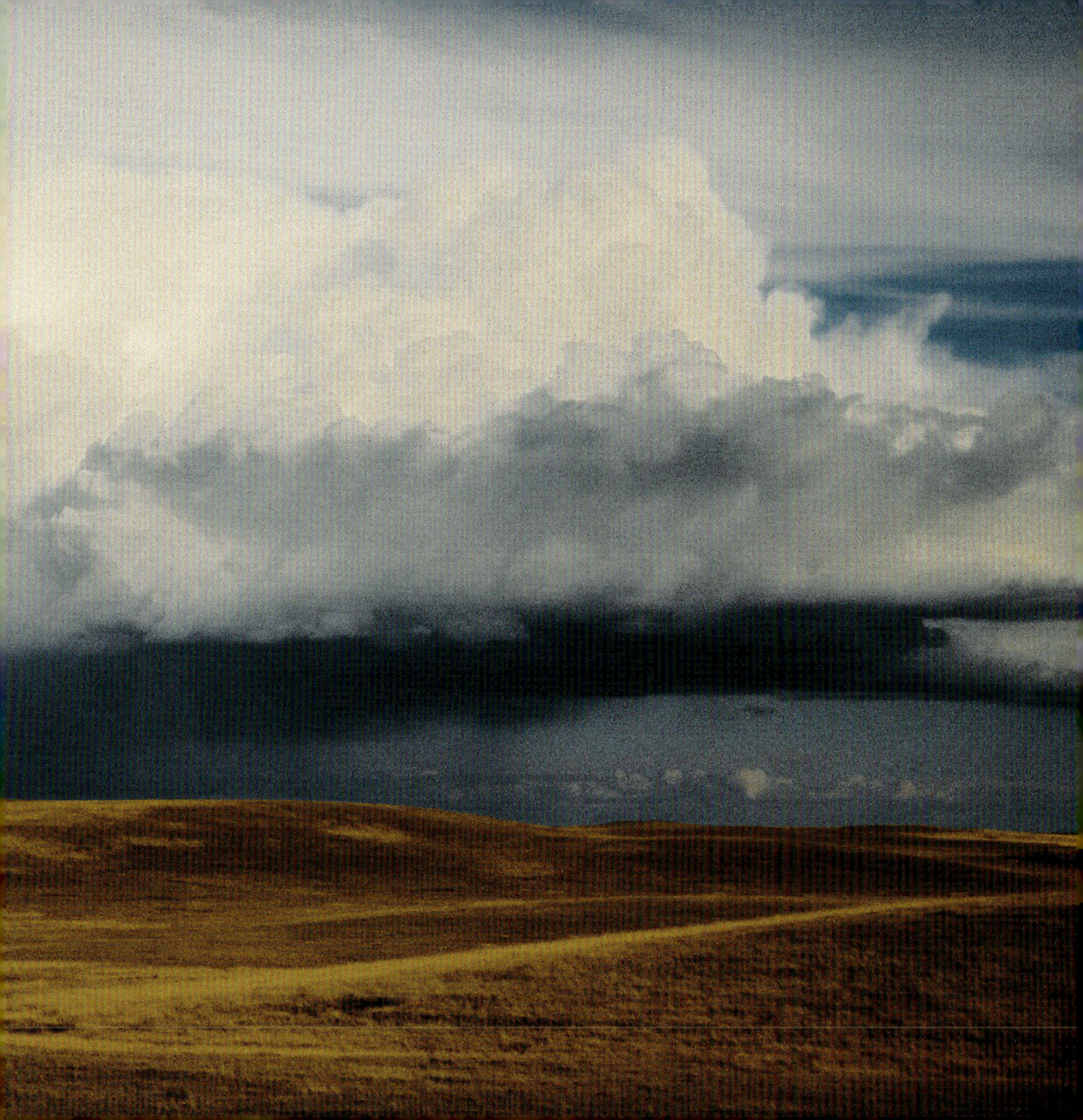

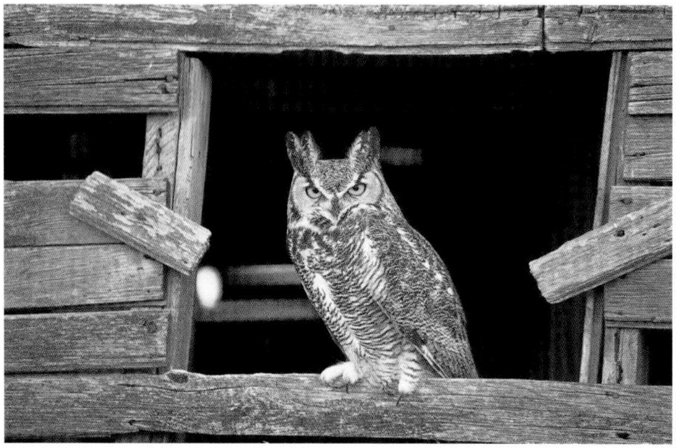

A Dream

Since his early twenties, Peter was beginning to understand that this nearly 13,000 acres of native grass—the rest was cropland or seeded to exotic species of grass—should remain as such, because of its intense beauty, and because, riding it from spring to fall, day after day, year after year, he had come to understand his grassland as ecologically fascinating and, as it disappeared all around him, an increasingly precious property. In order to keep its beauty, he began a policy (according to provincial government guidelines) of radically understocking it, thus keeping his grass in unusually good condition. Around him, over the years, the dynamic was such that unploughed land was under intense pressure to be farmed, and that, should he fail and have to sell, almost certainly the ranch would be subdivided, parts of it heavily grazed, and much of it, if not all, ploughed and seeded to crops. He began to try to think of ways, when the land would inevitably leave his control, to save the native grass—as an undivided large parcel—from destruction.

For years he simply thought about it, the idea growing stronger in his mind, his determination taking firmer and firmer hold. As he approached

Old homestead buildings provide shelter to the great horned owl.

retirement we began to contact various agencies, none of which were able to assist us. Finally, in 1993, we discovered the Nature Conservancy of Canada, with headquarters in Toronto and branches in the provinces. Although we had approached other agencies, either they showed no interest or indicated that they hadn't the funding for such a large project. The Nature Conservancy of Canada, an agency that searches out wilderness or near-wilderness areas, and organizes attempts to save them, then manages such lands using the best science available for their intrinsic natural values such as the preservation of biodiversity, and recognizing the needs of future generations, met our needs exactly. We wrote a letter expressing our desire to come to an arrangement whereby the Nature Conservancy might preserve the Butala land in its present state. Excited by the prospect of saving so much native grass, the Nature Conservancy of Canada began to search out ways to do so. Because so much of the land belonged to the province, the government had first to approve the project.

The provincial government, however, in choosing to facilitate the establishment of the OMB, would be "breaking trail" for future Saskatchewan governments, and thus needed to evaluate every aspect of the proposal in light of its mandate as guardians of the land, including considering the needs of future generations of Saskatchewan people. All the various government departments involved in establishing the conditions under which this conservation area could come into being—Sask Agriculture and Food, which makes agricultural policy for the province, Sask Environment and Resource Management or SERM, which among other duties manages Crown lands, the Farmland Security Board, and various sub-agencies such as the wildlife branch, the lands branch—acted with admirable promptness, efficiency, and foresight in considering the proposal, and eventually all agreed that the project should proceed.

Given that all available land is under extreme and continuing pressure to be cultivated or used as grazing land with a higher animal-to-land ratio than Peter had kept, a recommendation was introduced that its agricultural

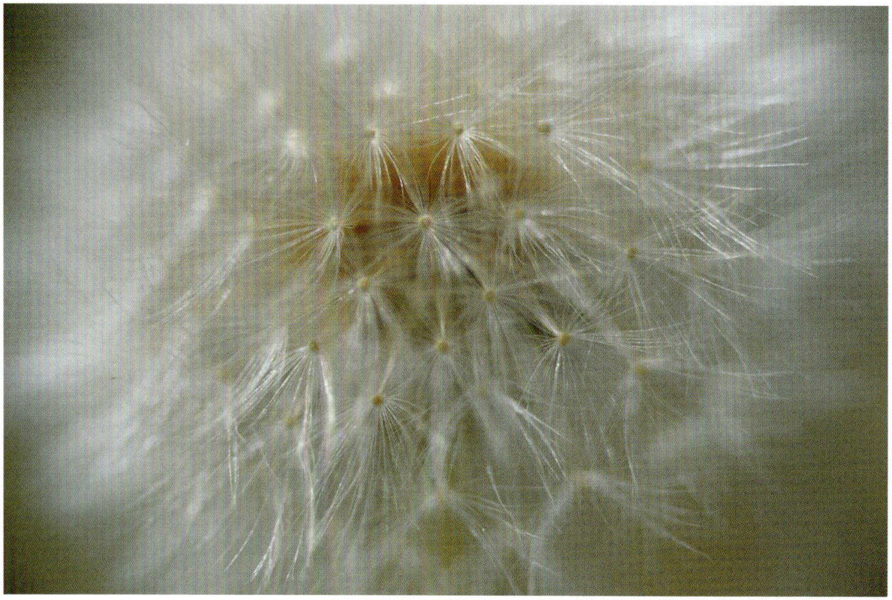

These feathery goatsbeard seeds are easily caught by the wind.

productivity should be maintained. The condition of Peter's grass when SERM and the Nature Conservancy of Canada took over was officially "excellent." In practical terms, this meant that the Nature Conservancy would be able to carry on an agricultural practice on the OMB, and yet do no further environmental damage. It meant also that the OMB would remain a working ranch.

Everyone involved in the project, which includes a local advisory board on which all partners in the enterprise sit, saw this requirement not as a limitation but as an exciting opportunity to do serious research into how these two situations—working ranch and conservation area—can be compatible. The OMB would also be a laboratory and a demonstration project, in fact, the largest such project in Saskatchewan, and the second largest in Western Canada.

One by one the reports of various scientists came in and the committee read and discussed them. Slowly, a consensus began to be reached. The OMB would become in part a bison preserve; the 1,200 cultivated acres would be restored to prairie; experiments would be done to discover the best way to stop the invasion into native prairie of Crested wheat grass (a plant from Siberia introduced to the Canadian prairies in 1915); plans would be made for a controlled tourism component. But at the same time, the OMB would continue to be a valuable wintering ground for the native pronghorn antelope which still inhabit it in fairly large numbers. It would also provide native habitat and a safe site for endangered ferruginous hawks, burrowing owls, in fact, for any of the thirty-four species of birds found on the OMB, including the "at risk" loggerhead shrike. And best of all, it would still be a mixed-grass prairie preserve.

This would be a return of sorts, the best version that can so far be managed in a land now inhabited and owned by an agricultural people. The bison would return, allowing us the joy of experiencing what we have only seen in tribal memories or in our dreams, and the wildlife—what is left of it—that once co-inhabited the prairie will return too.

On July 18, 1996, the Old Man On His Back Prairie and Heritage Conservation Area was dedicated with a celebration on the OMB itself, followed by a supper and evening of speeches and entertainment at Claydon Hall, the community centre five miles east of the OMB. The event at the hall was replete with government officials, Nature Conservancy of Canada people, representatives of funding agencies, and a number of other guests from as far away as British Columbia and Nova Scotia, plus many residents of the surrounding community.

The people of the Nekaneet reserve were invited to take part in the celebration as an acknowledgement of their history with the land, and the belief that only they could truly bless such an undertaking: an attempt to ensure that it would never be damaged or disturbed, all the land's memory erased, its beauty destroyed. The Nekaneet people saw that, within their spiritual system, certain ceremonies did indeed need to be conducted on the land itself, and to that end, a few days before their ceremony, an Elder drove out to choose the best place to hold his peoples' rites. He chose a location at the top of a high

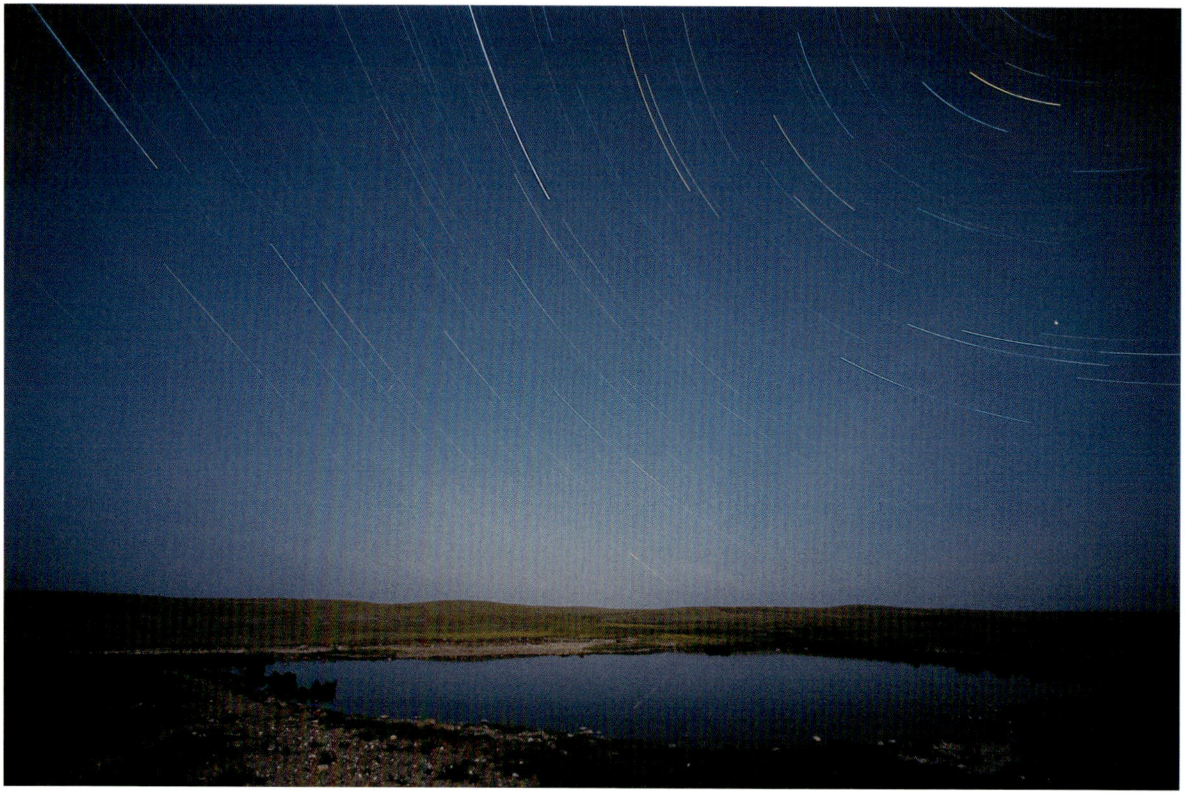

The tracks of the stars across the night sky during a two-hour exposure respond in kind to the mystery of the prairie.

hill from which the view is far-reaching in three directions and on which there are at least two unusually large, ancient stone circles. Then he left.

But not before he had answered the puzzled question of the non-Aboriginal man driving him: *Do you know anything about this strange name, Old Man On His Back?* "Why, yes," the Elder replied, without hesitation. "It got its name when a long time ago we found an old man up there, in bad shape."

As long ago as 1888, the Dominion of Canada map showing the Mounted Police patrols in the western District of Assiniboia called the OMB plateau the "Old Man On His Back", indicating that the name indeed comes from a time before there were settlers in that area, and that as early as 1888, it had been translated into English possibly from the Cree language, as the

Elder's "we" indicates. If there was any doubt, the name irrevocably determines that before the advent of Europeans the land of the OMB was Aboriginal land, well known to them, their territory as hunter-gatherers, in fact, their homeland.

At Christmas of 2001, the Nature Conservancy of Canada officially took control of the OMB. Today, the Nature Conservancy of Canada and SERM, and their numerous partners, have the difficult but joyful task of stewardship of this priceless land. Peter Butala has become one of the lucky few in the world whose fondest dream—and far, far more, he says—has come true.

The questions this grassland by its very wildness and beauty—the sense it gave me of being itself *present* or intelligent—first caused me to ask are not fully answered. I suppose that in this life they never will be. But I have been taught enough to understand that there are reasons that far outweigh the gathering of wealth that require humans to preserve in an undisturbed state places like the Old Man On His Back Prairie and Heritage Conservation Area.

Wilderness, it turns out, is an absolute value in itself. It is our last connection with creation and, as such, contains all possibilities for life. We human beings know in our bones and our blood that we need it, that it contributes to our happiness, to our sense of belonging on this earth. Perhaps most important of all, its existence reminds us of our spiritual nature, of what it is to be human, of where we have come from and where we are going when we die. In such a sense, land is holy; it is sacred. And it belongs to all of us.

It is time all of us who know about the profound beauty and hope, about a kind of salvation that is to be found in nature, joined together—both mystics and pragmatists—with a new land ethic designed to achieve a way of life that recognizes our *kinship* with the rest of nature, that recognizes, at last, that wilderness is the source of our human-ness and that without a vibrant and living *natural* planet, we cannot survive.

Following page: The unfulfilled dream of the people of semi-arid lands—abundant water.

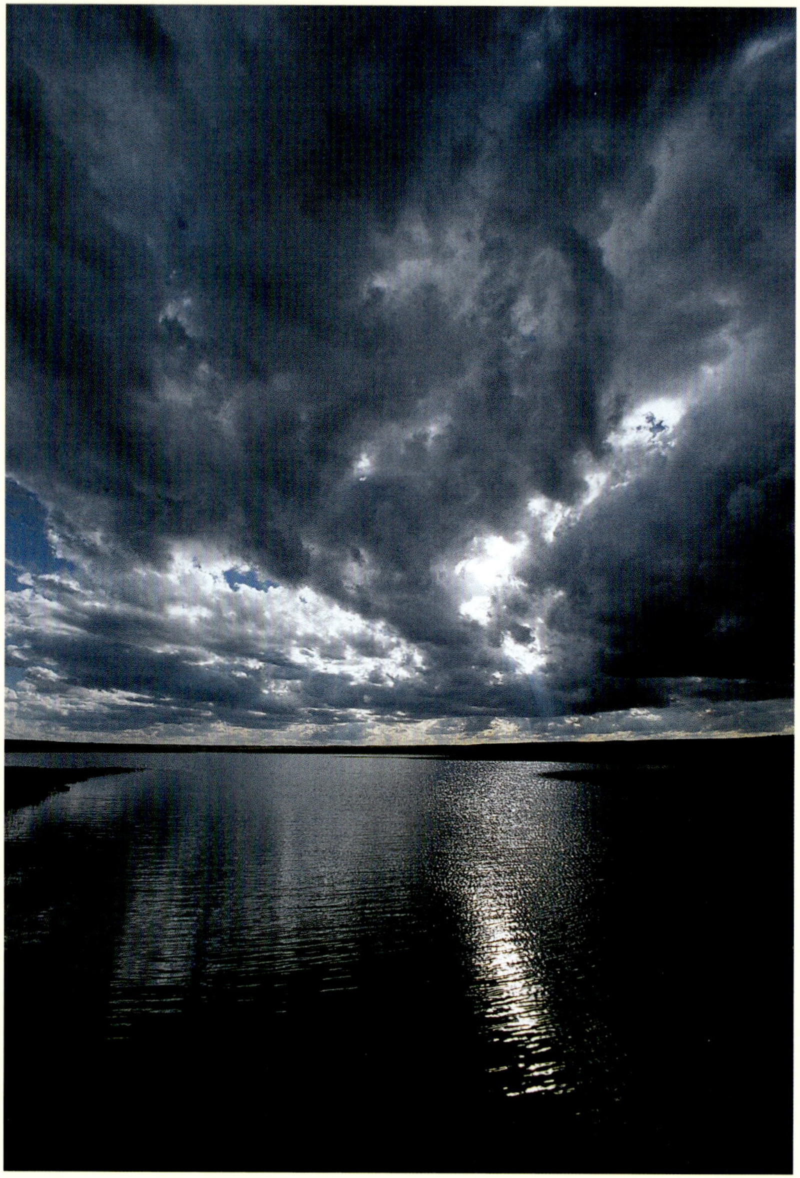